Freire and Children's Literature

T0002853

FREIRE IN FOCUS

Series editors: Greg William Misiaszek and Carlos Alberto Torres

This series of short-format books provide readers a diverse range of Paulo Freire's work and Freireans' reinventions toward social justice both inside and outside education, without readers needing any prior knowledge of his scholarship. The books offer new perspectives on the work of Freire's teaching, ideas, methods, and philosophies. Each book will introduce Freire's work so it is easily understood by a wider audience without overly simplifying the depth of his scholarship.

Advisory Board

Also Available in the Series

Forthcoming in the Series

Freire and Children's Literature

ERNEST MORRELL AND
JODENE MORRELL

BLOOMSBURY ACADEMIC
LONDON • NEW YORK • OXFORD • NEW DELHI • SYDNEY

BLOOMSBURY ACADEMIC
Bloomsbury Publishing Plc
50 Bedford Square, London, WC1B 3DP, UK
1385 Broadway, New York, NY 10018, USA
29 Earlsfort Terrace, Dublin 2, Ireland

BLOOMSBURY, BLOOMSBURY ACADEMIC and the
Diana logo are trademarks of Bloomsbury Publishing Plc

First published in Great Britain 2023

Series design by Charlotte James
Cover image © Paulo Freire via Torres, Carlos Alberto (2014). First Freire:
Early writings in social justice education. Teachers College Press.
Background image © ilyast/Getty Images

A catalogue record for this book is available from the British Library.

A catalog record for this book is available from the Library of Congress.

ISBN: HB: 978-1-3502-9223-9
         PB: 978-1-3502-9224-6
       ePDF: 978-1-3502-9225-3
      eBook: 978-1-3502-9226-0

Series: Freire in Focus

Typeset by Integra Software Services Pvt. Ltd.
Printed and bound in Great Britain

To find out more about our authors and books visit www.bloomsbury.com
and sign up for our newsletters.

CONTENTS

SERIES EDITORS' FOREWORD

Greg William Misiaszek

Paulo Freire emphasized that theories are useless without action. The book you have in your hands reinvents Freire's theories for critical, multicultural teaching through children's literature. Theories and scholarship guiding education must lead to students' and teachers' actions for bettering the world. The Bloomsbury *Freire in Focus* book series, in which this book is housed in, is an attempt to give readers short-length, easy-to-read books on using Freire's scholarship within teaching practices and beyond the education field. Carlos Alberto Torres and I hope the Series will widen readership and usage of Freire's work within and outside traditional "academic" spaces. We see Freirean-based reflexivity *with* practice as essential to make the increasingly globalized world more just, equitable, peaceful, innovative, and sustainable, among numerous other aspects that Freire emphasized as vital in re-making a "better world."

This book by Ernest Morrell and Jodene Morrell is a superb model reflecting Carlos and my initial discussions on the Series, which occurred in Mexico City in 2018. They use and reinvent Freire's work on teaching literacy for young students to read critically to connect their own lives and others' lives worldwide. In diverse ways, they argue teaching students to read the counterstories of children's literature that are often glanced over in traditional literacy education—the crucial and impactful, but often hidden, lessons written on the pages. For example, Ernest and Jodene discuss the need to read *behind*, *within*, and *in front of* the text, as they provide rich descriptions and examples for each type of reading. They argue the essentialness of multi-perspective, polyvocal readings in an increasingly multicultural world for teaching for social justice and other aspects previously listed. Within Freirean scholarship, this book helps fill the gap of utilizing his pedagogies within K-12 education settings, as Freire's work is too frequently miscategorized as only applicable to adult education.

Utilizing Freire and other critical literacy scholars' work, Ernest and Jodene problematize how humanized teaching through children's literature can lead to students' hope and love—self-love, love for one another, and love for the world overall. They brilliantly illustrate this and other arguments through richly detailed classroom vignettes at the beginning of and threaded throughout each chapter. They describe how teaching through children's literature is essential for achieving Freire's assertion that education should lead students to dream of utopias and provide them with the tools *to* reach them. Freire despised rampant fatalism within education that sustains and intensifies oppressions by having a false single future/fate they condemn to people. They advocate for childhood literacy education that encourages utopic reflexivity, which is essential for students' praxis. As Moacir Gadotti (1996) argues, praxis emerges through democratic, dialectical, and problem-posing education to unveil the gaps (or "limit situations" as termed by Freire) between current happenings and what ideally *should* be happening within foundations of social justice. Ernest and Jodene's descriptions of teaching through literature lead not only to young students being able to construct their own utopias but for their utopic constructions to be grounded in social justice from their reflexive readings. In turn, this social justice essence continues with students' praxis.

Although they give details on the selection processes of children's books, they also strongly argue that *how* children's literature is taught is often more important than *what* they read. For example, social-historical unpacking of literature is essential, as well as teaching these analysis skills to students as they read beyond those assigned. Children's literature can help amplify students' voices when read multiculturally, resulting in conscientization (conscientização) to better understand themselves, their communities, and the world's diversity. They point out that critically deconstructing books collectively uncover their intended, but often hidden, ideologies which frequently can be reinvented toward goals of justice, equity, and love through dialogue.

As advocated throughout this book, reading has students and teachers reinvent the books' words to be contextually meaningful to them. In addition, such reading points out oppressions and reflects upon possibilities for countering them. This includes announcing and denouncing injustices and stereotypes portrayed, which might not be challenged in the books' pages. Morrow (2019) describes Freirean reinvention as, in part, announcing and denouncing oppressions for reconstructing teaching that is meaningful and successful toward ending oppressions. This book embodies such goals of critical reinvention within the teaching and reading of children's literature, as the authors give examples of students' daily lives, such as bullying, to the world at large. They provide classroom examples of how literature can help young students to deal with hardships outside classroom walls, including death and violent crimes. These vignettes do not only describe teaching successes but also failures, such as teachers avoiding sensitive topics that literature often raises and dismissing necessary discussions literature (in)directly brings up (e.g., a student bringing up the subject of death who recently had a family member passing).

This book embodies Freire's literacy education goal of reading the word to read the world. Freirean-based teaching of childhood literacy is extremely important, as can be witnessed by Ernest and Jodene pointing out that children as young as two years of age make meaningful connections to literature.

This book is indispensable for anyone teaching through children's literature, both improving young students' reading individually and possibilities of transformations toward a better world collectively.

References

Gadotti, M. (1996). *Pedagogy of Praxis: A Dialectical Philosophy of Education*. SUNY Press.

Morrow, R. A. (2019). Paulo Freire and the "logic of reinvention": Power, the state, and education in the global age. In C. Torres, A. (Ed.), *Wiley Handbook of Paulo Freire* (pp. 445–62). Wiley-Blackwell.

ACKNOWLEDGMENTS

We are deeply grateful to the series editors, Greg Misiaszek and Carlos Torres, who we consider colleagues—but more importantly friends in this lifelong struggle for educational justice and pedagogies of love and freedom. We are thankful to the editorial team at Bloomsbury and the reviewers who helped us to convey our ideas through clear and heartfelt prose made stronger with their suggestions.

We are eternally grateful to the students and families who welcomed us into their learning environments and lives over the past thirty years. We feel privileged to share the fruits of this inspiring and collaborative literacy work, which aims not just to improve skills that are measured and treasured in school, but to manifest self-actualization and enact social change.

We are thankful for the Center for Literacy Education (CLE) which is made possible by the support of the University of Notre Dame—specifically the Institute for Educational Initiatives and the College of Arts and Letters Department of English. The CLE has allowed us the time, space, and inspiration to reflect on our scholarship, gather and revisit existing publications, write timely and original text, and attempt to move the field of literacy education forward with this book.

Several chapters are reprints. We are thankful to the editors who graciously agreed to allow us to reprint the originals or versions of the work. Chapter 1, "Becoming Powerful Readers of the Word and World: Multicultural Readings of Children's and YA Literature" first appeared as a white paper, "Becoming Powerful Readers of the Word and the World," White Paper (originally from MyPerspectives 2022 Teachers Edition Grades 6–12 by Ernest Morrell and Jodene Morrell © 2022 by Savvas Learning Company LLC). Chapter 2, "Multicultural Literature and the Promotion of Social Awareness in ELA Classrooms" was originally published in the *New England Reading Association Journal* in 2012. Chapter 3, "Linking the Word to the World: Connecting Multicultural Children's Literature to the Lives of Twenty-first Century Youth" originally appeared in *Dragon Lode* (Copyright 2021). Chapter 4, "Student Voice and Agency in the Polyvocal Literature Classroom," first appeared in *English in Texas* 51(1), pp. 11–15. (Copyright 2021 by Texas Council of Teachers of English).

Finally, we are indebted to our family members—those who came before us and those who come after us. You have given us the privilege of time, access, and insight to merge our love of learning, freedom, and literacy to hopefully inspire others and make the world a more welcoming and supportive place where every person can grow and thrive in revolutionary love.

Introduction: Freirian Approaches to Teaching Children's Literature: Joy, Voice, Agency, Responsiveness, and Love

Belonging and the Beloved Community

A group of fourth graders have just finished reading Christopher Paul Curtis's Bud Not Buddy *as part of a unit titled* Belonging and the Beloved Community. *In addition to the chapter book their teacher has brought in elements of popular culture including television, film, social media, music, and photographs of Michigan in the 1930s and 1940s. The students have worked in groups asking and answering critical questions about race, culture, and belonging in twentieth- and twenty-first-century America. They have particularly honed in on the myriad ways that contemporary media have created divisions among people and how those divisions have caused conflict and hurt. They've also examined ways that storytelling can change how we think about the past, how we think about ourselves, and how we think about each other. For the final project the students are developing transformative media campaigns that deal with the issues of family, community, and love. Some students are focusing on self-love and ideas about beauty; others are focusing on the language of division and hate. Some are focused directly on the media itself and how their peers can become better consumers of the media. The genres are varied. Some students are using Scratch to create their own video games, others are writing their own hip-hop album, and still others are working on podcasts that they plan to share with other classes at school. A final group is developing an eco-friendly concept for public spaces in their postindustrial town. As she looks at the buzz of excitement in these nine- and ten-year-olds, the teacher reflects on her own journey that began a half decade ago in her first teacher preparation class where she asked how the work of Paulo Freire might influence her approaches to teaching children's literature. She smiles to herself as she rushes to a group with raised hands.*

As Paulo Freire stated so powerfully nearly fifty years ago, the central problem his work attempted to tackle is dehumanization, a lack of self-love. Reading the first sentence of *Pedagogy of the Oppressed* thirty years ago as beginning teachers in Oakland and San Francisco, the words and works of Paulo Freire became the framework of the practices we are proud to share in this volume. Paulo's work speaks to the transformative power of an approach to teaching and learning centered around voice, agency, joy, responsiveness, and love. It's not that educators tell students that they are loved or hated, this is rare. It's that we create opportunities for young people to be heard and to be actionable in the world around them. That young people are fully humanized in the work that is demanded of them. What they are called to do. So much that happens in institutionalized instruction can make children feel smaller than they already see themselves. A Freirian approach begins with the fully actualized subject. A child in this case, who feels important and impactful.

We'll speak to how a Freirian-inspired pedagogy of children's literature can help to make that happen.

The pedagogy of children's literature is deservedly becoming a hot topic of study in university settings and in professional development and for good reason. Teaching young people how to become readers of the word and the world is one of the more important things we do in classroom life. We generally teach reading through engaging literature for children. Literature exposes children to the world of ideas, it allows them to learn about their place in the world. Literature presents a set of value propositions for children to grapple with, some good and some not so good for them. Literature can also excite the mind and the creation of the stories that children want to tell about their own hopes and dreams. But it is this act of reading, of being able to decode the word and the world that is the passport to informed and engaged citizenship, the joy of the active and encompassed mind that is the Holy Grail of elementary and secondary classroom instruction of which children's literature, the teaching of children's literature, holds center court.

We wrote this book to explore Freirian-inspired pedagogy and culturally responsive instruction as meaningful ways for parents, teachers, and community leaders to engage children's and young adult literature. Collectively, the chapters focus on five core theories: joy, voice, agency, responsiveness, and love. When students experience *joy in learning*, they develop confidence. This is critical because the most destructive enemy in education is self-loathing, which is connected to a lack of confidence and interest which leads to a lack of motivation. We address self-loathing by providing high interest work to build students' confidence and elicit joy. Children's literature provides a powerful means to incorporate student choice each day. We can also support students in creating and enacting world-changing action projects to bring joy to learning.

Voice, which is often coupled with choice, serves as a refrain throughout the entire book. Voice means encouraging and supporting students to speak in languages that matter to them, helping them to become powerful interlocutors in polyvocal classrooms and, ultimately, in the larger world. This concept of voice is closely connected to Youth Participatory Action Research (YPAR), which emphasizes the importance of having students participate in various learning modalities such as large group discussions, small group discussions, and independent projects. Voice is also connected to the kinds of writing students do. Voice is an interwoven fabric, through which children's literature serves as a gateway to storytelling. This happens when students create their own stories, write screenplays and films, write and draw their own manga and comics, or become graphic artists.

Agency is concerned with engagement and action. Most children's literature from the nineteenth century to the present offers some type of value proposition whether it's bullying or oppression or simply feeling small in the world. At the end of most children's literature is some kind of action that kids want to take. Freire (1970) calls this coalescence of informed action and reflection "praxis," which is an ideal modality for learning in the classroom. Students reflect on the ideas in the book but they can also take some form of action whether it is in the community, creating a work of art, engaging in dialogues and conversations, and inventing those multiple and varied actions which may often emanate from the intersections of children's literature with calls for agency. Connecting the reading of literature to writing and social justice is an incredibly important component of the pedagogy we and others advocate (Torres, 2014).

We are not teaching literature per se, we are teaching children through literature. Hence, *responsiveness* is the fourth concept framing our book. We know that responsive instruction begins with questions that stem from students' interests so we need to make sure that we have libraries that reflect the tapestry of the human condition.

The final concept, woven throughout every chapter, is *love*. If the enemy is dehumanization, then the project is humanization. How do we manifest love? We manifest love by helping children feel powerful and efficacious. We do not simply tell them they are loved. We put them into situations where they can manifest the love they have for the world, which is the beauty of this approach. Rather than thinking about *doing for people*, we need to focus on *doing with people* with love. The key component of love is solidarity—solidarity with students and supporting students to be in solidarity with their communities. Teaching with a Freirean approach is animated by love for the students, especially making and remaking the word and the world through love.

In addition to the five concepts (joy, voice, agency, responsiveness, and love), we aimed to closely examine how a Freirian-inspired critical pedagogy can influence the teaching of literature for children and to focus on important but less frequently discussed aspects of literacy education including— polyvocality, student voice, critical family engagement, popular culture, and multicultural readings of literature connected to children's literature. To achieve these ends, we lay out a five-part approach to theorizing a critical pedagogy of children's literature that draws on: (1) Freirean critical pedagogy, (2) culturally responsive instruction, (3) sociocultural theory, (4) social and emotional learning, and (5) New Literacy Studies. We discuss some of the high-leverage practices connected to this work such as culturally responsive read alouds, the engagement of youth popular culture, critical media literacy development, student voice and agency, and the development of world-changer projects using a youth participatory action research approach.

Critical pedagogy, or education intended to promote self-awareness, inspire consciousness and action for change, has the potential to become one of the most relevant and powerful tools in literacy education today. Our five-part approach to theorizing a critical literacy pedagogy begins with the work of Brazilian educator Paulo Freire. There are many ways into the work of Paulo Freire and we have written of him often (Duncan-Andrade & Morrell, 2008; Morrell, 2008), but we'll start this conversation by identifying Freire's work as the practice and theorizing of a pedagogy of self-love and social transformation.

Paulo Freire was astute in recognizing the power of language, media, and schooling in shaping a mindset that perpetuated social inequality (Freire, 1970). Prior to external social action, Freire identified the first steps as internal, interrupting deficit mindsets through consciousness-raising, problem-posing, and the development of a critical literacy, or an ability to read the word and the world (Freire & Macedo, 1987). A new reading of the word and the world not only allows the critical subject to separate themselves from deficit language and ideologies, but also allows a re-languaging, or a creation of new narratives that are affirming, inclusive, and empowering. We believe that the critical teaching of children's literature will create spaces for the young people in our classrooms to critique deficit narratives while also exposing them to humanizing literary stories as they do the work of articulating their own realities and making their voices heard.

Freire also viewed literacy as preparation for a self-managed life with three goals of education: (1) to self-reflect ("know thyself"), (2) to become aware of the forces that rule individual's lives and shape their consciousness, and (3) to set the conditions for producing a new life, "a new set of arrangements where power has been, at least in tendency, transferred to those who literally make the social world by transforming nature and themselves" (Giroux, citing Aronowitz, 2009). A Freirean critical pedagogical approach is concerned with transforming the ways we see ourselves and the world, and our power to exist on our own terms and challenge inequitable and oppressive forces in the pursuit of social justice (Torres, 2014).

Culturally responsive instruction, which emerged in the 1970s as a response to the civil rights movement, is crucial to consider when we ask about how to reduce racial, religious, and/or gender prejudices partly through providing a framework for a critical questioning of texts and the world (Banks, 1978). A critical aspect of culturally responsive instruction is to introduce students to other voices, reduce prejudice, and see ourselves as part of a collective humanizing, making critical questioning and cultural confidence equally important. We adamantly believe that all students can become more engaged with responsive instruction. This means being simultaneously responsive to all of our students' needs, interests, and their voracious capacity to learn and grow. Toward these ends we promote a culturally responsive instruction that honors choice and voice. We will say much more about this in our chapter on the polyvocal classroom. We draw on the work of culturally responsive instruction and multicultural education in making the case for multicultural readings of literature, for the reading of authors across multiple dimensions of diversity, and for promoting student voice in what we call "The Polyvocal Classroom."

Sociocultural theory, which considers how social interactions and cultural interaction inspired powerful learning, emerged from the renewed interest in the work of Lev Vygotsky in the 1970s (Vygotsky, 1978). Learning scientists at the time questioned how parents, caregivers, and communities created powerful spaces for learning outside of the classroom. These educational scholars (i.e., Scriber & Cole, 1981) acknowledged that children come from cultures and communities with tremendously valuable knowledge. Instead of assuming students are tabula rasas when they begin formal schooling, these scholars and educators argue that we need to make meaningful connections to their provocative and informative outside worlds (Gutierrez, 2008). Tapping into their funds of knowledge or community cultural wealth means thinking about the community as having valuable knowledge (de los Rios, 2019; Moll, Gonzalez, Amanti & Neff, 1992; Solórzano & Yosso, 2002). Ethnographers of literacy drew upon sociocultural theory to document the important literacy practices that occurred in homes, churches, neighborhoods, and popular culture (Alim, 2006; Fisher, 2007; Heath, 1983). We have drawn heavily upon sociocultural theory to make connections between the teaching of literature in classrooms and the powerful literacy practices that youth and their families are involved in outside of the classroom.

Social and emotional learning theories are interested in helping all students to develop a sense of self and social awareness

(Selman, 2003), to have a sense of themselves as empowered individuals, to learn to get along with others and participate meaningfully in communities, and to envision themselves as able to contribute to the transformation of the world. These ideas of self-love, self-awareness, and generating intercultural dialogue are interrelated and prevent alienation, isolation, and self-doubt while promoting active communal learning and a global perspective. Allyn and Morrell (2022) identify the need for a three-part focus on self, community, and world in their social and emotional learning (SEL)-based strengths framework for children's literacy development. Students need to see themselves as belonging to a community of literacy learners; they need to have their curiosity acknowledged as they ask big questions of literature and the world around them. They need to learn to practice friendship and kindness as members of a community. They need to learn to become listeners and interlocutors within diverse communities of learners. Finally, they need to develop the confidence and courage to see themselves as world-changers and to participate in the work of transforming the world around them. We also draw on these ideas as we consider how the critical teaching of literature can help students to develop an understanding of self, an understanding of others, and an engagement with the social world.

Finally, *New Literacy Studies*, inspired by the work of the New London Group in the 1990s (New London Group, 1996), examines how changes in technology are changing the ways that young people practice literacy, in their consumption habits (video games, music, film, the Internet) and especially their cultural production. New technologies have given young people much more agency in how they can use literacy skills to create and share information. Much of the scholarship of NLS documents the creative ways that young people are practicing literacy in the digital age (Barton and Hamilton, 200; Gee, 2003; Lankshear & Knoble, 2003; Street, 1984). All school-age students, from Kindergarten to high-school seniors, were born in the twenty-first century and only know a world with the Internet and constant connection. We have an entire generation of young people for whom the new literacies are not new at all. It is all they know. How can that inspire us? For all who remember a pre-digital world, we can think about our current moment and how we accommodate our students' perspectives and experiences within the work we do. The confluence of technology and literacy has become more mainstream over the past twenty-five years within a framework of digital literacies in the twenty-first century, but the mainstream movements often lack the criticality or the focus on youth agency that is a hallmark of New Literacy Studies. We will draw on New Literacy Studies and the idea of a critical digital media literacy (Kellner, 1995; Morrell, 2008) to expand our conceptualization of literature for children to include video games, anime, manga, music, film, and youth popular culture more generally.

We would be remiss to discuss a rapidly changing world full of challenges and possibilities without acknowledging the impact the Covid world pandemic has had on families, schools, and the field of education. In the following chapters, described in further detail below, we are mindful of the ways the pandemic has shined a blinding spotlight on inequities, making this book even more pressing for a rapidly shifting educational landscape. As previously stated, we propose using literature to create classrooms filled with joy, motivation, engagement, achievement, and relevance; and to be adults who promote active learning that stimulates curiosity, creativity, and the social awareness needed to foster kindness, courage, and hope—both inside and outside of the classroom. We thus believe a Freirean approach to teaching literature is a viable and powerful means.

Chapter Overviews

We begin the book with the chapter, *Becoming Powerful Readers of the Word and the World: Multicultural Readings of Children's and YA Literature*. We draw on one of Freire's highly recognized pedagogical approaches to developing critical consciousness, voice, and agency through a literacy practice of reading the word and the world. Specifically, we focus on multicultural readings of literature, regardless of the genre or modality, to increase students' joy, engagement, and achievement. We argue that when students understand the social and historical contexts of the authors and the texts they read, they are able to read the texts closely and critically for what is explicitly stated or what is silent or absent. When they are able to unpack potential biases, and when they are able to act in the real world as writers, thinkers, and change agents informed in their actions by their critical perspective, they can fully engage in a multicultural reading of texts. We draw on the work of Henry Giroux (1990) to discuss a three-part approach to multiculturally reading children's and young adult literature: (1) reading behind the text (author centered), (2) reading within the text (text centered), and (3) reading in front of the text (reader centered). Through this approach, students bring their own perspectives along with those of critical literary theory to substantively and seriously engage the canonical and contemporary texts they read.

In Chapter 2, *Multicultural Literature and the Promotion of Social Awareness in ELA Classrooms,* we build upon the urgings of early scholars in the field of children's literature (Charlemae Hill Rollins, Rudine Sims Bishops, Virginia Hamilton, and Walter Dean Myers) to provide opportunities for students to powerfully engage a multicultural literature that affirms their sense of self and promotes an agency in the world around them while also fostering the development of academic language and literacies. In many ways the work of African American children's literature scholars like Chicago Public Librarian Charlemae Hill Rollins (1897–1979) anticipates and complements the work of Paulo Freire and more well-known critical pedagogical theorists. Whenever possible we try to create lines of synergy between these less well-known African American pedagogical theorists and those who are more often cited in the academic literature. Drawing on these critical scholars of children's literature, we argue that students need access to diverse texts as well as a critical reading framework that allows them to bring multiple perspectives to any texts they read. We call this idea multicultural readings.

Similar to Chapter 1, we focus on the importance of making powerful connections between the word and the world in Chapter 3, *Linking the Word to the World: Connecting Multicultural Children's Literature to the Lives of Twenty-first Century Youth*. Specifically, we draw on Paulo Freire and Gloria Ladson-Billings who both encouraged educators to embed classroom practices in the everyday experiences of students and create lessons that increase cultural competence among historically marginalized students. While we recognize that teachers are often pressured to focus on testing and quantitative measures of students' success, we argue that academic achievement is often a result of motivation, engagement and relevance, as well as other qualities that are difficult to quantify such as curiosity, creatively, kindness, courage, and hope (Allyn & Morrell, 2016). We offer examples of literacy practices that link the teaching of literature to the worlds of our students and how this relates to text selections, reading, and writing.

Polyvocality, or the equitable presence of multiple voices engaged in human dialogue, is the focus in Chapter 4, *Student Voice and Agency in the Polyvocal Literature Classroom*. Classroom talk, particularly in small and whole group discussions, is critical to facilitating literacy growth, nurturing relationships, and building students' confidence in the classroom. Encouraging classroom talk also helps students to hone their active listening skills, which helps to build more powerful learning communities. We look beyond the confines of a polyvocal classroom to helping all students become mindful and empowered contributing members of families, communities, and the global public sphere. As in other chapters, we provide examples from the classrooms—in this case multimodal projects and presentations. More importantly, we discuss ways to incorporate classroom talk into everyday literacy instruction to create a responsive learning environment where every student's voice is heard, valued, and celebrated.

In the fifth chapter, we turn our attention to students' homes and families with *Critical Family Engagement in Reading Multicultural Literature*. While family engagement has always been an important component of students' academic success, the COVID pandemic has blurred the line between home and school by forcing teachers and schools to depend even more on families to support students' learning. We suggest a critical framework for family engagement that honors and responds to students' and families' needs and interests by including interactive culturally responsive literacy activities such as read alouds and independent reading time based on students' choice. We revisit and emphasize the importance of multicultural literature from earlier chapters, and draw on relevant research to discuss the importance of out-of-school reading practices and offer ways that educators can engage parents as partners and encourage and support joyful reading and storytelling at home. Finally, we discuss Family Literacy Nights framed in a strength-based approach to help every child become a Super Reader (Allyn & Morrell, 2016) by nurturing social-emotional development at home and school.

The final chapter aims to highlight the importance of a Freirean approach to teaching literature beyond traditional literacy skills measured and treasured in schools and to focusing on joy, voice, responsiveness, antiracism, and revolutionary love in everyday literacy practices. As the title states, *The Future of Children's Literature Is Already Here*, all we need to do is tap into and bring children's worlds into the classroom—whether this is in the form of various genres and platforms such as video games, graphic novels, anime, manga, gaming, and in other forms of literacy rich popular culture and digital media. Children and young adults are marinated in words and images—our challenge and opportunity are to capitalize on their existing strengths, interests, and gifts to be critical consumers and producers in the world. We highlight throughlines across chapters including multicultural readings of all texts, reading the word and the world in student practice and teacher planning, student voice, and blurring the lines between school, home, and community. We aim to support, challenge, and invite all educators to make their classrooms literacy- and literature-rich environments that capitalize on the strengths and passions of their students to help all students become powerful and empowered change agents in the classroom and beyond.

CHAPTER ONE

Becoming Powerful Readers of the Word and the World: Multicultural Readings of Children's and YA Literature

A class of fifth graders just watched a powerful read aloud on YouTube from Sankofa Read Aloud (an Online African American Children Stories website) of Derrick Barnes's Crown: An Ode to the Fresh Cut. They are now in small groups and each group is looking closely at a copy of the physical text. One group excitedly points out the stickers on the cover—Newbery Honor Book, Caldecott Honor Book, Coretta Scott King Honor Award, and Ezra Jack Keats Book Award—amazed that one book received so much recognition. Another group is looking at the illustrations by award-winning artist Gordon C. James and marveling at the brilliant colors, the vivid expressions on the characters' faces, commenting on how some of the characters look like people they know. A third group is talking about how they know Derrick Barnes has four sons so perhaps that's why he wrote this book, and many of his other books, about African American boys. The last group is still talking about the YouTube video and how much they liked the way the narrator read the book—exactly as it is written on the page and with so much emotion—like people at their local barbershop. After a few minutes of discussing their initial responses to the picture book, they focus on their task at hand. One group is using Chromebooks to "read behind the text" which entails searching for information about Derrick Barnes, information about the book, reading book reviews, researching key events in 2017 when the book was published and reading the "Note from the Author" on the last page of the book. Another group is engaged in a close read of the text—studying the style of the writing, discussing the genre and how it is a "slice of life" book (Bishop, 2007)—something many children experience in their "regular life." They also notice the use of Black English and the celebration of Black life and culture for a "within the text" reading. Another group is discussing how some people might not like the words in the book because they don't appreciate or understand some of the terms and phrases such as "That's my word" or "It hooks up your intellectual" or words like "nope," "yeah," "shout out, "dude," or "locs." They also recognize how this book challenges negative dominant narratives about African American communities, in their own fifth-grade discourse they are "reading in front" of the text. After twenty minutes, the groups reconvene as a whole class and share their findings from their three approaches to reading the text to contribute to a deep, multicultural reading of Crown: An Ode to the Fresh Cut.

There is often a conversation in English Language Arts about the selection of children's and young adult literature with an eye toward adding what we call diverse or multicultural texts. We translate that to mean that we want authors from the past and present who represent a wide range of lived experiences, as well as cultural and linguistic heritages. While we would stop short of classifying some authors as multicultural and others as "mainstream" we do agree that diversity and difference, as they cohere across a group of authors, are important. And underrepresentation and misrepresentation of certain authors and groups need to be addressed in the literacy classroom. The purpose of this chapter, though, is to ask a different question about the texts we choose to teach to children and adolescents. It isn't *what* we teach, but *how* we teach the texts we choose to teach. More specifically, how should we read *all* children's and young adult literature multiculturally?

The multicultural reading approach we present in this chapter is very much inspired by the work of scholars Gloria Ladson Billings (1994) and James Banks (1996) who both see as key principles of their work having students empowered to ask critical questions of the written word and the world around them. Ladson-Billings argues for a three-part approach to culturally relevant pedagogy that includes academic excellence, cultural competence, and critical consciousness. Banks (1996) offers five dimensions of multicultural education, which include: (1) content integration; (2) the knowledge construction process; (3) prejudice reduction; (4) an equity pedagogy; and (5) an empowering school culture and social structure.

Drawing on the frameworks of Ladson-Billings and Banks, multicultural readings of literature should increase student joy, engagement, and achievement (Allyn & Morrell, 2016), they should reduce prejudice, they should develop critical consciousness, and they should promote equity and intercultural understanding across multiple lines of difference. We argue in this chapter that multicultural readings of texts can achieve these ends when students possess the ability to understand the social and historical contexts of the authors and the texts that they read; when they are able to read the texts closely and critically for what they say and what they leave silent or unsaid; and when they are able to unpack potential biases; and, finally, when they are able to act in the real world as writers, thinkers, and change agents informed in their actions by their critical, multicultural readings of texts.

We are also inspired by the work of Freire and Macedo (1987) and other critical literary theorists that demand that older readers look at texts and the world from a variety of perspectives, whether that be intersectional, reader response, postcolonial, or new historical (Appleman, 2015; Wilhelm, 2016). Rather than limit young readers to a handful of critical literary approaches, we instead present a framework for questioning texts that brings in historical, formalist, and critical approaches to the study of literature.

Ultimately, we advocate for a three-part approach to multiculturally reading children's and young adult literature which we will explore in subsequent sections of this chapter; reading behind the text, reading within the text, and reading in front of the text. Ernest was first acquainted with a three-part approach to reading cultural texts through the work of Henry Giroux (1990) and began immediately to think about how to utilize Giroux's framework to help his students read literary texts in the K-12 classrooms where he taught in Northern and Southern California. While Giroux advocated for reading upon, within, and against the text, Ernest thought of inviting students to read behind, within, and in front of the text; bringing in their own perspectives along with those of critical literary theory to substantively engage the canonical and contemporary texts that they read seriously. The reading in front is less of a confrontation than it is a dialogue out of what Nobel Laureate Toni Morrison in *Playing in the Dark: Whiteness and the Literary Imagination* (1992) calls a deep admiration and respect for what authors craft. Our three-part approach to multicultural readings is also formed by Aristotle's rhetorical triangle (the three rhetorical appeals) which focuses on *logos* (text-context), *pathos* (audience-reader), and *ethos* (author). Inspired by Aristotle we also look at reading behind the text as an *author-centered* approach, reading within the text as a *text-centered* approach, and reading in front of the text as a *reader-centered* approach.

Reading Behind the Texts

When students read behind the text, they focus on the author by asking questions such as "who is the author" and "when did he or she write the text"? By starting with these questions, students learn more about the experiences of the author and how these may have shaped how and what the author chose to write. By understanding when the author wrote the text, students are thinking about social, political, and cultural factors that may have influenced the author's choices. When reading behind the texts, students consider the "implied reader," or who the author may have been imagining as their audience and how their audience's values and beliefs may have influenced their decisions about what to write and how to write.

Students should also question the purpose of the text. Scholars such as Sutherland (1985) suggest that all authors bring their ideologies to their work and often this falls into one of three types of political stances: (1) advocacy: "pleading for and promoting a specific cause, upholding a particular point of view or course of action as being valid and right" (p. 2); (2) attack: essentially the opposite of advocacy—"generated by the authors' sense of amusement, outrage, or contempt when they encounter something that runs counter to their concepts of right and wrong, good and evil, justice, fair play, decency, or truth" (p. 4); and (3) assent: "does not advocate in any direct sense, but simply affirms ideologies generally prevalent in the society" (p. 7). In essence, authors write to persuade their readers to share their perspective as to what is right and good (advocacy), to reject what they view as wrong (attack), or to assent to dominant narratives whether these are beneficial or harmful to certain groups or society as a whole.

Finally, students can learn more about how the text was received at the time it was written. One measure of a response is whether a book appears on a banned book list, such as the frequently updated list available on the American Library Association website. Opposition is often initiated and supported by parents and librarians who believe certain books are inappropriate for children. These reactions to a text can tell us a great deal about the dominant social and cultural values at the time of publication. We can also have students think about how texts are received differently by children and adults, what is considered award winning versus what is most popular with children, which can be quite different. Key questions one might ask from a reading behind the text approach include:

- Who is the author?

- When did he/she write the text?

- What historical or contemporary events would have influenced the construction of the text?

- Who was the immediate audience of the text? What were/are the beliefs, values of the audience? How did/do they see the world?

- What purpose did the text serve?

- How was the text received? What, if any, were the debates or contentions around the text?

A behind the text approach can contribute to a multicultural reading because it shows students that all texts are written from a sociohistorical location. All authors are, in a sense, biased. They are all members of cultural communities, they hold viewpoints, and they write, as they see the world, from a particular point of view. With a behind the text reading, even young students are able to see culture at play in the construction of the text and they are also able to juxtapose their own social location against that of the authors of the texts they study.

Reading Within the Texts

The second approach is reading within a text. When students engage in this type of reading, the text becomes the focus and students can pose questions about elements of the text. For example, if the text is a narrative, students can investigate the plot, characters, and setting. They can identify specific evidence in the text to understand the historical, social, gender, cultural, racial, religious, and/or political life of the times portrayed in the text. Often the time period is different from the time of publication and students should understand that social, political, and cultural norms may have been different. An example of this is Mildred Taylor's *Roll of Thunder, Hear My Cry* which is the story of the Logan family in 1930s Southern Mississippi. The book was published in 1976, so readers would need to understand how many African Americans, like the Logans, experienced everyday life in the South, which was significantly different from the time of publication. Another example of the importance of historical, social, cultural, racial, religious, and political life of the time is Pam Munoz-Ryan's novel *Echo*, which weaves together three very distinct cultures, experiences, and places—a boy in Germany in 1933, two white orphaned boys in Philadelphia in 1935, and a Mexican American girl in her immigrant community in Fresno County, CA in 1942. Students would need to understand the historical context of each place—such as the domination of the Nazis in Germany and segregated schools in California for Mexican American children to make sense of the characters' experiences.

As students are asking questions about and considering these elements of the text, they might dig deeper to identify who speaks and who is silenced and how this reflects the values and beliefs at the time of publication or setting of the text. Likewise, they should consider the social languages used to communicate within the text, such as among characters, as well as to the reader (the author's writing style). Often when a less familiar dialect is used, such as Middle English in Geoffrey Chaucer's *Canterbury Tales*, readers are forced to slow their reading pace to ensure they understand the text. For younger readers, this could be a character such as the cabby in C. S. Lewis's *The Magician's Nephew* (Book #1 in the Chronicles of Narnia) who speaks with an old London cockney accent. In other texts, authors may choose to use less "mainstream" or "dominant" dialects or to weave in various languages. One example is the way Munoz-Ryan weaves in Spanish words and phrases in her novel *Esperanza Rising* or to have the same text written side by side in English and Spanish such as Carmen Lomas Garza's book, *En Mi Familia*. This style of writing may force some readers to slow down whereas other readers may feel validated and elated to see their own dialect or language in print. With this approach to reading, the text becomes centered and students draw heavily on the printed text to support their claims and analysis and focus on the author's style and craft.

Key questions one might ask from a reading within the text approach include:

- What happens in the text?

- Who are the characters? What takes place in the text? Where does the action take place?

- Who speaks and who is silenced?

- What social languages are used to communicate?

- What are the features of the text?

- What evidence can we find in the text of the historical, social, gender, cultural, racial, religious, and/or political life of the time?

- How is the text structured? What is its style?

A "within the text" approach can contribute to a multicultural reading because it shows students that texts often fit in particular genres because of their characteristics. For example, informational texts use specialized language characteristics such as general nouns and timeless verbs and does not utilize characters through the book (Duke & Bennett-Armistead, 2003); however, the authors, illustrators, and publishers make choices about which topics and whose biographies are worth telling and if images of people are included, whether they represent a wide range of cultures, phenotypes, socioeconomic backgrounds, and so on. Likewise, narratives typically include a plot, setting, atmosphere, characterization, theme, point of view, and figurative language and literary devices. How authors address these seven elements can contribute to a multicultural reading if their characters represent a range of cultures, ethnicities, languages and dialects, socioeconomic backgrounds, political views, and religions, and are portrayed in authentic positive ways free of stereotypes and essentialized simplistic caricatures (Thomas, 2016).

Reading in Front of the Texts

The third approach places the reader at the center. As they read, students are asking about biases in the text and how certain readers may find the text problematic. Students should consider contradictions or debates that the text has generated or is likely to generate as well as alternative readings or interpretations of the text. One well-known example of this would be Mark Twain's *The Adventures of Huckleberry Finn*. First published in the United Kingdom in December 1884 and two months later in the United States, Twain wrote the novel as a satire with its blatant use of racist and coarse language and glaring critique of slavery and racism. While some read the novel as racist, which was not what Twain intended, others were able to identify the ways in which Twain was critiquing slavery as a socially accepted system at the time of publication. As students read a text, such as *The Adventures of Huckleberry Finn*, they should be asking how gender, race, culture, or politics affect how readers might respond to the text. They can think about when the text was initially published versus when they are reading and how these might be extremely different.

With this third approach, readers can think about how the text provokes and inspires new thinking and action. An excellent example of this is Kwame Alexander's award-winning book (Caldecott Winner, Newbery Honor, Coretta Scott King, Golden Kite) *The Undefeated* which is described as "a soaring tribute to the enduring perseverance and achievements of the past and a stirring call to action to 'the dreamers and the doers' of the present and the future" (School Library Journal). Breathtaking illustrations by Kadir Nelson celebrate highly recognized individuals such as Dr. Martin Luther King, Jr. as well as families, children, a soldier—and a heart-wrenching black and white image of hundreds of enslaved Africans laying side by side on a slave ship. The book is ultimately a celebration of hope, persistence, and strength and Alexander ends the book with the phrase "this is for us." This poetic picture book is an example of a text that provokes and forces readers to acknowledge the past, to celebrate one another, and to act with hope in solidarity with others.

Key questions one might ask from a reading within the text approach include:

- What are biases in the text?

- How might certain readers find the text problematic?

- What contradictions or debates has the text generated or is likely to generate?

- What are alternative readings or interpretations of the text?

- How might gender, race, culture, religion, or politics affect how readers might respond to the text?

- How might the text provoke or inspire new thinking and action?

Critical literary theories offer opportunities for reading in front of the text. The reading in front of the text is really the payoff for a multicultural reading. As a reader-centered approach, students are able to levy a cultural critique upon the texts they read; really upon all texts that they confront with the class and outside of class. Students can champion those texts that they feel uplift or are inclusive and empowering. They can call out bigotry, insensitivity, racism, sexism, homophobia, and anti-religious bias. Imperfect texts are not a problem for the ELA classroom. Again, we are reminded of Toni Morrison's *Playing in the Dark* where she applauds generative authors for being willing to take chances and share with us their imperfections. The imperfections in texts only become a problem when students are not encouraged to call them out. We critique, Morrison argues, as an act of respect. As an act of joy.

Reading in front of the texts can also be a vehicle to real action in the world. With culminating projects, students can engage in youth participatory action research, where they investigate real-world issues (Mirra, Garcia & Morrell, 2016), they can become authors of their own creative texts, and they can become literary critics who ask deeper questions of the literature they read and share these analyses with other students and literary scholars around the world. For example, Ernest was recently approached by a high-school student who had created his own literary journal that employed university professors as referees and discussants of student-created literary works and literary criticism. The journal was publishing its third issue and had already recruited distinguished faculty from the most prestigious English departments around the country. This is just one of numerous examples we could share of how students can use their voices to impact the world when we create spaces for them to develop the skills and confidence to speak the truth to power and to share their diverse perspectives with authentic audiences. Nothing confers a sense of agency and value like being listened to by others.

Multicultural Approaches and the Joy of Reading the Text

We are at a moment where we have a real opportunity to reshape our children's and young adolescent's relationships with the texts they read that increases students' reading identities, that enhances their joy of reading, and that recenters the power relationship between students and all of the texts that they read. We are reminded of the work of Louise Rosenblatt (1904–2005) who in *Literature as Exploration* (1938), argued that truly powerful reading happened when the reader and the text met in a space she called the "poem." Reader-centric and text-centric approaches paled in comparison to her transactional model of reading. We feel that this could very easily apply to our three-part approach to multicultural reading of children's and young adult literature. The cultural responsiveness, the power and joy, all happen in the transaction that is guided by the critical questions we empower our students to ask. When bolstered by polyvocal classrooms that honor student voice and student perspectives, we feel that the conditions are ideal for increasing academic achievement, intercultural and social awareness, and an enduring love of language and an appreciation for the very hard and very important work that writers do.

While the focus of this chapter has been on teaching our K-12 students to read all texts from a three-part approach (reading behind: author centered; reading within: text centered; reading in front: reader centered), we recognize the importance of teacher educators adopting this same critical multicultural reading of their own texts. Scholars Botelho and Rudman (2009) call this approach a critical multicultural perspective, meaning we attend "not just to its literary quality as art but also to issues of power and representation of people of various cultural backgrounds" (p. 7 cited by Martínez-Roldán, 2013). The demographics of elementary teachers continues to be 80 percent female, white, and middle class, which is significantly different from the 54.1 million children in American schools who are now more than 54 percent non-white (NCES, 2022). Given the demographics of the majority of teacher education students, we should be asking the same questions and reading behind, within, and in front of texts. What are authors assuming about the "typical" teacher education student's lived experiences, perspectives, social/cultural/political views, and how these may shape their assumptions about children and literacy pedagogy? Are authors assuming readers bring deficit perspectives about their future or current students and communities, an outsider's stance, or other negative dispositions? What might this mean for the 20 percent of teacher educators who are members of historically marginalized and parallel cultures (Hamilton, 1989) they teach? What are the implicit and explicit messages in the texts and how can educators identify, embrace, or push back?

CHAPTER TWO

Multicultural Literature and the Promotion of Social Awareness in ELA Classrooms

A midsized urban school district in the Midwest purchased copies of Sid Fleischman's Seedfolks for every middle-school student. The Literacy Specialists from each school compiled a binder of resources and suggested novel study strategies for all middle-school teachers. Each school committed to spending two months on the novel study. Once the unit is complete, each student will have participated in creating a school community garden and an additional project, of their own choosing and design, to beautify their neighborhood. In a sixth-grade class, in a school that partners with Refugee Services, there are twenty students representing ten birth countries and ten different home languages (English, Somali, Spanish, Vietnamese, Arabic, Kurdish, Haitian-Creole, Dinka, and Swahili). They are discussing the opening paragraph of the vignette, "Wendell" in Seedfolks which reads, "My phone doesn't ring much, which suits me fine. That's how I got the news about our boy, shot dead like a dog in the street" (p. X). One of the students raises his hand and recounts seeing a dead body in the street in his home country. He talks about how people stepped over the body and how upsetting it was for him and his family. Other students are quiet, some are nodding their heads. One student raises her hand and asks, "Did you know them?" The student responds that he did not. Another student asks, "What happened to him?" The student is not sure. The teacher, a young woman in her second year of teaching, tells the student that she is very sorry that he had to experience these types of events and asks how his family coped with these occurrences in their home country which was experiencing political turmoil based on hundreds of years of tension between two countries. Some of the students who were coming from war-torn countries nodded and shared similar stories. Many of the students who grew up near the school listened respectfully and asked sensitive questions. After several minutes, the teacher thanks the students for sharing, tells them they will finish reading the vignette and encourages them to continue to share their personal connections to the text as they read. The following day, the teacher begins class with an "aesthetic quickwrite" which gives students time and space to write and process their own emotions and memories in relation to the text before launching into their small group discussions, then reading the next vignette as a class. The teacher remains at the periphery of the room to give students space to share with one another, knowing they will have time to share in their whole group discussion. She is grateful that the district chose this multicultural literature given the demographics of her class and the type of conversations sparked by the vignettes which has encouraged students to be listeners, interlocutors, and empathetic friends.

Even at the tender age of two, children can make meaningful connections to literature. One of our child's favorite books, *Busy Toes* (Bowie, 2002), features African Diaspora children using their toes in amusing and creative ways. Midway through the book is an illustration of a toddler with skin tone, hair texture, and facial features similar to his. Each time we turned to the page featuring this child, our son would point and excitedly repeat, "That's me!". Recently, a ten-year-old student saw a copy of Derrick Barnes's *Crown: An Ode to the Fresh Cut* sitting on our home desk. He grabbed the book, held it up to his face and said, "He looks like me!" Indeed, the image of the child on the cover with his beautiful brown skin and curly faux hawk looked just like this child. As in the previous example, we snapped a photo, sent it to his iPad, and proceeded to read the book together.

Children are constantly looking for what Bishop (1990) calls "mirrors" on the cover and in the pages of books. They are also looking for multicultural literature that features "windows" and "sliding glass doors" about children, places, and experiences different from their own that broaden their understanding of the world. Making connections to literature can begin at a young age and with thoughtful and careful planning, we can provide many opportunities for our students to connect with multicultural literature, in ways that affirm their sense of self, their awareness of the world around them, and their connection to academic language and literacies. In this chapter, we draw on the humanizing pedagogy of Paulo Freire and others to make the case for centering multicultural literature in English Language Arts classrooms. Further, we argue that students not only need access to diverse texts, but also need a set of reading skills that allow them to bring multiple cultural and critical perspectives to any texts they read. What we called in the previous chapter *multicultural readings*. Finally, we offer several examples of how we and our colleagues have attempted to enact a pedagogy of multicultural readings of multicultural literature.

The Importance of Multicultural Literature in Today's Classrooms

According to the Center for Public Education, with birth and immigration trends, soon there will be no majority ethnic group in the United States (www.centerforpubliceducation. org). In 2022, 57.8 percent of the population is White alone (non-Hispanic); however, this has decreased from 63.7 percent since 2010. The second largest racial/ethnic group is the Hispanic/Latino population (Jensen et al., 2021), comprising 18.7 percent of the total population and 28 percent of the K-12 student population (NCES, 2022). More specifically, the disaggregated data for 76 of the largest city school districts in the United States, which serve 8.2 million students, is 44 percent Hispanic, 27 percent African American, 18 percent White, 8 percent Asian/Pacific Islander, and 2 percent Alaskan/Native American. Sixteen percent are English Learners, 71 percent are eligible for free/reduced price lunch, and 15 percent have Individualized Education Programs (Council of Great City Schools, 2021). Based on the most recent available data from 2019, 12.3 million students attended high-poverty schools. When disaggregated by school locale, 40 percent were in city schools, compared to 20 percent for town schools, 18 percent for suburban schools, and 15 percent for rural schools (NCES, 2022).

But these numbers are not just occurring in our "urban schools." It is important to understand that diversity is everywhere. Nationally our schools are already 54 percent non-white and according to the National Center for Education statistics, these trends are expected to continue (NCES, 2022). And while for these introductory statistics we've focused on racial and ethnic diversity, our classrooms also have religious diversity, socioeconomic diversity, diversity of family and home life, and diversity in language and country of origin to name a few. Given the diversity of our K-12 student population and the importance of children both seeing themselves and various perspectives through the texts that they encounter in school, powerful teaching of multicultural literature can empower individuals and transform beliefs. And the idea that multicultural literature is most appropriate or only useful for children of historically marginalized groups is now outdated (Landt, 2007). This is not a new or recent concern. In Nancy Larrick's 1965 article "The All White World of Children's Literature" in the *Saturday Review*, she stated that, "Across the country, 6,340,000 nonwhite children are learning to read and to understand the American way of life in books which either omit them entirely or scarcely mention them. There is no need to elaborate upon the damage—much of it irreparable—to the Negro child's personality." She went on to state, "… the white child learns from his books that he is the kingfish. There seems little chance of developing the humility so urgently needed for world cooperation, instead of world conflict, as long as our children are brought up on gentle doses of racism through their books." Dr. Rudine Sims Bishop, leading scholar of multicultural children's literature, most well known for her analogy of multicultural children's literature as windows, mirrors, and sliding glass doors (1990) has continued to make this argument—that diversity needs to go both ways. In a video for Reading Rockets (2015), she argued that multicultural literature is "not just for children who have been underrepresented and marginalized"; rather it is also for the "children who always find their mirrors in the books and therefore get an exaggerated sense of their own self-worth and a false sense of what the world is like because it's becoming more and more colorful and diverse as time goes by."

Weaving multicultural literature throughout the curriculum has the potential to promote cultural pluralism and challenge assimilation to dominant belief systems and canons of knowledge (Yoon, Simpson & Haag, 2010). This, we believe, is a benefit to all students at a crucial moment in their lives when they are learning to accept themselves and to understand others. From a broader perspective, incorporating multicultural literature fulfills the purpose of multicultural education, which is to help students "critically analyze their cultural, social and political worlds and understand pluralistic perspectives of different cultures in the minority groups" (Yoon, Simpson & Haag, 2010, p. 110). This is very consonant with Freire's (1970) concern that true education begins with the present, existential, concrete situation, reflecting the aspirations of the learner. It is in this situation that we begin our engagement with children and multicultural literature. While there are

various definitions of multicultural literature, when broadly
defined, multicultural literature is about people from diverse
cultural, linguistic, socioeconomic, and religious backgrounds,
who have been marginalized, and are considered outside of the
mainstream of society.

High-quality multicultural literature should offer authentic
representations of marginalized groups and their experiences
and "showcase beliefs, perspectives, and experiences previously
overshadowed by dominant communities" (Graff, 2010,
p. 107). Essentially, multicultural literature should acknowledge
and celebrate multiple dimensions of diversity while
challenging and dissolving stereotypes. While our examples
focus specifically on African American children's literature, we
can still draw on Bishops' (1982) description of three types
of literature: (1) social conscience—literature written by and
for whites to elicit empathy, sympathy, and tolerance, (2)
melting pot—for both African Americans and non-African
Americans to celebrate universal similarities, and (3) culturally
conscious—reflecting the distinctive cultural and social aspects
of growing up Black and American. We can substitute what
Virginia Hamilton (1989) called any "parallel culture" (various
cultures living parallel and equal rather than "minority") for
African American or Black, but the gold standard remains
culturally conscious multicultural literature.

Multicultural literature for children and young adults
grew during the eras of racial, ethnic, and gender civil rights
in the 1960s and 1970s. During the next two decades,
multicultural literature was narrowly defined as literature
by and about people of color. Since the 1990s, the term has
broadened to include people who have been misrepresented
and underrepresented to also address issues related to gender,
sexual orientation, and disabilities (Yokota, 2001). While some
texts may be labeled multicultural, readers should consider
the authenticity and accuracy of the content and whether the
inferred messages are challenging or promoting misconceptions
of a particular group. For example, in a review of multicultural
picture books, researchers found that several books that were

categorized as multicultural promoted assimilation rather than pluralism (Yoon, Simpson & Haag, 2010), which is contrary to the purpose and goals of multicultural literature and multicultural education. In a similar example, Chen (2009) discusses children's and young adults' books about Chinese people and culture and how researchers have found erroneous representations of Chinese culture from mixing Asian cultures, a heavy emphasis on Ancient China rather than modern history, and a narrow focus on folktales as opposed to current narratives. We still find many books featuring Asian characters as recent immigrants, thereby promoting the "perpetual foreigner" stereotype, ignoring recent data showing that one in three Asian American and Pacific Islanders were born in the United States and approximately 45 percent of foreign-born Asian Americans and Pacific Islanders have lived in the United States for more than twenty years (New American Economy, 2021). Equally problematic is treating groups of people as homogenous or assuming they all share the same experiences (Gutierrez & Rogoff, 2003, cited by Martínez-Roldán, 2013). Similar to how Asians have been treated in literature, we see similar misrepresentations of culture and language in books that include inaccurate and disrespectful portrayals of Latinos and Spanish speakers. Dr. Carmen Martinez-Roldan, a leading scholar of teaching and learning in bilingual contexts and young Latino students' literacy/biliteracy development, has written about the misrepresentation of Latinos in literature that fail to promote cultural understandings and avoid stereotypes, especially by cultural outsiders. In particular, she has addressed the *Skippyjon Jones* series as problematic because of its use of "Mock Spanish" (register of Anglo Spanish used mostly by Anglo speakers of English when addressing one another), using a chihuahua to represent Mexican Americans, and perpetuating negative and racist stereotypes of Mexicans and other Latino groups. Whether the author is aware of "parodic use of language and misrepresentation of Mexicans is irrelevant" because the consequences are the same—harming children's self-image and hindering learning, respect and appreciation for other cultures and languages (p. 12). By considering the broad definition of multicultural literature, and being aware of how cultures and languages can be (mis)represented in literature, educators can make informed decisions on which texts to include in their curriculum for the benefit of all students.

How We Read Literature

When we talk of multiculturalism and its applications for the study and teaching of literature we are simultaneously focused on the choice of texts and the choice of readings of the text. Too often, we fear, multicultural literature is narrowly defined by either the author or the subject of the text. If, however, these "multicultural" texts are taught in culturally alienating ways, what good have we done? The same students who have been marginalized from the dominant ways of schooling will continue to feel marginalized while reading authors of diverse backgrounds. A colleague of Ernest's often talks about an African American literature course that was taught at a diverse metropolitan high school. Despite the large percentage of African Americans attending the school, only one was enrolled in the African American literature course. This young woman often talked to the adult researcher about not feeling as if she had an authentic voice in the class and she frequently wanted to drop the course. The choices of literature didn't make her feel any more connected to the course because the structures didn't change. Ultimately this young woman did leave the course and this particular school was forced to reconcile the reality that its African American literature class enrolled no African Americans.

There is another story that bears telling here. Again, Ernest was working at a different diverse metropolitan high school where students were reading *Huck Finn*. The demographics of the class were reflective somewhat of the schools' diverse racial and socioeconomic composition. Early in the book the subject of race emerged. Not just the use of the "N" word, which is prevalent in the story, but just generally whether race was a salient issue in the novel. The discussion, which featured only one turn by a non-white student, ultimately decided that neither the N word or race were significant issues that needed to be discussed in the class's reading of the text. While the teacher disagreed, she ultimately acquiesced to the students' desires. When Ernest queried the students who were silent (he had been working with many of these students on a two-year project) each of them vehemently disagreed with the assessment that race was not a major issue in the novel, yet they did not know how to bring their own experiences or a racialized perspective to the reading of the book, so they sat silently as the issue was dismissed by their classmates.

Each of these anecdotes bears some importance to this idea of promoting multicultural readings of multicultural texts. While a text may lend itself to an analysis that centers upon race, gender, or difference, it will ultimately be the teaching of that text that truly enables students to read the text multiculturally if you will. Along the same lines, students should feel the right to bring their experiences and perspectives to bear on any text that they encounter in school (Rosenblatt, 1978). While *Huck Finn* would not be considered by most as a multicultural text, clearly students wanted to bring their multicultural perspectives to the analysis of the text. An added space for this sort of reading would have, in our opinion, increased engagement and ultimately understanding of the book.

Students bring their multiple cultural perspectives with them wherever they go and these perspectives allow them to read with and against the texts they encounter. This has to be taken into consideration when we ponder a theory of reading that accompanies our ideas about inclusivity, solidarity, and awareness. Along these lines when we think about multicultural readings of texts we should encourage students not only to tap into their own cultural reservoirs, but also to practice reading texts from the perspectives of others. One concept in an elementary literature curriculum encourages students to step into someone else's shoes. This is an idea that even very young children will understand. When advocating for critical literary theory in middle and secondary instruction Deborah Appleman (2000) makes the same argument. She acknowledges the importance of reader response theory, but makes the argument that it can limit students to only read texts from their own perspectives, particularly when these perspectives can perpetuate inequality. Therefore, in promoting a multicultural theory of reading multicultural texts we advocate for a multiperspectival approach that allows students to consider issues of oppression, marginalization, and resistance in all texts that they read that allows them to draw both on their own cultural reservoirs of knowledge, and from empathy and solidarity with the experiences of others. We return to the strength-based approach to literacy of Allyn & Morrell (2016) to consider how a critical pedagogical approach to children's literature can foster a better understanding of the self, of others, and of the world.

Multicultural Literature and the Promotion of Social Awareness

Understanding Myself

One of the most important things we can do for our students is help them to understand themselves better as they come to a larger understanding of the world around them. As Henry Louis Gates Jr. has written, we sometimes use literature to write ourselves into being (Gates, 1992). Through encountering stories that serve as a mirror into our own lives, we come to understand ourselves better as we read and react to the stories of others who have had similar fears, joys, and experiences. This is only possible through a rich and diverse selection of literature that allows students to encounter many points of view. Reader response theory also provides an important connection between the world of multicultural texts and the worlds of our students (Wilhelm, 1997). As our students encounter these provocative stories of others, we also allow them to insert their own stories into the conversation and through gaining a greater understanding of the text, ideally they come to a greater appreciation of their own voyage through life.

Understanding Others

It is also important, however, for students to understand and accept others. Our schools and our society are very diverse places and in order for us to have the kind of mutual respect and understanding needed for a peaceful and vibrant civil life, people need to come together across multiple lines of difference. They need to be able to listen, to respect different perspectives, and to appreciate all that diversity has to offer. And this is not something that should begin in adulthood. As teachers of children, we can find ways to promote the understanding of others in our primary grade curricula, and multicultural teachings of multicultural literatures is one way of developing that sort of cultural competence.

Understanding the World

As students are simultaneously using the reading of literature to understand themselves and others, these students can also be encouraged through the study of literature to take a broader and more agentive view of the world. That is, the study of literature can foster awareness and "tolerance"; specifically, Freire's critical expression of tolerance which is "founded on the basic human principles of respect, discipline, dignity, and ethical responsibility" (Darder, 1998, p. 508). Most importantly, the study of literature can foster action upon the world. For instance, when reading about bullying or the long-term implications of environmental waste, students might be encouraged to think about how they can employ their own words in the service of societal improvement. We have both witnessed classrooms where students wrote plays, poems, newsletters, and editorials to elected officials based on conversations and activities that grew out of literature-based units. In one specific example, third graders in Southern California read *The Story of Ruby Bridges* by Robert Coles and then created their own skit where they focused on the ways that society had improved since that time as well as areas where they thought we still needed improvement. As part of a youth summit presentation, these third graders also created a PowerPoint presentation where they shared research they had done on the conditions of their local schools and neighborhoods fifty years after the Bridges incident.

A Literature Pedagogy of Social Awareness

Attachment Theory

For healthy development and to develop social awareness, young children need their primary caretaker(s) to provide safety, security, and protection. According to Mary Ainsworth and John Bowlby, leading theorists of attachment theory, the most critical time for attachment between children and adult(s) is six months to two years of age (see Bretherton, 1992). During this time, their biological aim is survival while their psychological aim is security. Attachment theory is most often associated with young children; however, older children may experience similar negative responses from prolonged absence, breakdowns in communication, emotional unavailability, or signs of rejection or abandonment from the adults in their lives. Given the extensive amount of time students spend in the classroom, we can draw on attachment theory to understand the importance of positive and nurturing relationships between students and their academic world. As institutions charged with the care and development of youth, schools need also consider the importance of creating spaces for students to form powerful attachments with their teachers, their peers, with academic content, and with the world at large (Dewey, 1901; Selman, 2003).

Attachments to the Academic World

Much of what applies to attachment theory and the importance of caregivers can translate to life in classrooms and schools. In fact, we know that at the upper grades, the primary reason for dropping out of school is that students feel no attachment to the school or any of its staff (Marcus & Sanders-Reio, 2001). Having just one person at a school that cares and reaches out can make the difference! But this is true throughout the educational spectrum. If they are truly to develop as intellectuals and self-actualized literate beings, students need to be able to form meaningful attachments with the academic world. This means making attachments to their classroom teachers and classmates which we will talk about in a moment, but we argue that this also means making an attachment in general to the world of school including the environment, the curricula, and the ways of being that are associated with school life. We believe that encouraging multicultural readings of multicultural literature in an open and humane environment that promotes understanding and awareness can foster this important attachment. Students are more likely to see themselves and their stories represented in a diverse curriculum, they are likely to see their ways of understanding and interpreting the world (i.e., using popular culture, oral history), and they are more likely to be able to express themselves and their opinions via meaningful discussions and through classroom projects that allow them to critique existing texts and to create and share their own multimodal texts.

Attachments to the Literary World

Promoting multicultural readings of multicultural literature can also aid in fostering attachments to the literary world. By this we mean several things. First of all, through the wonderful available literature students will literally be able to attach themselves to the characters, the stories, the places, the languages, and the experiences of those in the literature that they read. A monocultural reading list only allows a subset of students to do this. But this shouldn't mean that students only see themselves in literature that reflects their nationality or ethnic background. Through reading approaches that empower students and their perspectives, students should feel that their experiences can be brought to bear on the reading of any text and they should be encouraged to make connections between their world and the world of the story. *After all, who hasn't wanted to bake an Enemy Pie (Munson, 2000) for a foe or rival?*

Attachments to Others in My Classroom

Children and adults want to feel valued as a member of a community. Helping children to find commonalities with their peers and teacher to nurture meaningful attachments can be fostered through the use of literature. Through shared readings, teachers and students can identify similar experiences that may not come up in everyday conversations. For example, while reading Fleischman's *Seedfolks* with sixth graders, we discovered that many of the students translated for their non-English speaking parents and struggled with the shift in power and roles that this responsibility brought. Students who were not expected to translate empathized with their peers and asked thoughtful and sensitive questions about how this impacted their identity. Similarly, while reading Fleischman's *The Whipping Boy*, the class of third graders were incensed by the injustice of a whipping boy taking the punishment for the misbehavior of a spoiled prince. They sympathized with the character and shared how they would feel if they were the whipping boy. In another read aloud, seventh graders were horrified by the way Maleeka, the protagonist in Flake's *The Skin I'm In*, is mistreated by others due to the color of her skin and her socioeconomic status. With each of these books, students focused on the characters' experiences, but their conversations created opportunities to share their own experiences and perspectives with one another, thereby creating a more humane and close classroom community. Conversations often began with how it would feel to step into the shoes of the character to how it felt to experience a similar injustice, which brought students together and strengthened personal attachments within the classroom.

Attachments to the Larger Social World

Spend time with young children and you are bound to hear the question, "Why?" Children are inherently curious about the world and their place in it. They are constantly developing and modifying schemas to make sense of new information and how it relates to them. As previously discussed, children also seek connections with individuals and the social circles in which they travel. Literature can help children to expand their perspectives and schemas and discover their personal connections to ideas, social worlds, and people beyond their immediate tangible surroundings.

For children, making self-to-text and text-to-text connections are easier than making text-to-world connections due to their developing understanding of the world beyond them (Tompkins, 2006). However, when using multicultural literature to teach third-grade Social Studies, as opposed to a textbook, Jodene found that the literature was a powerful tool for helping students connect to the past and present, make connections with people and places, and consider issues of social justice. To learn about the history of Los Angeles, our larger surrounding community, we read Bunting's *Smoky Night*. The students were too young to remember the 1992 Los Angeles riots, but while reading the book together, we discussed issues of power and justice and why people might resort to violence. Students assumed various characters' roles and how they might have felt as the main character, an African American boy named Daniel, or Mrs. Kim, whose market is ransacked during the riots. With another book, *The Wonderful Towers of Watts*, students learned about the Watts Towers, which we discussed in relation to the history of Watts. The book resonated with students because their community was often described in deficit terms but they knew of talented, socially minded community members who cared about their neighborhood and strove to make it better—similar to the artist of the Watts Towers. The last book which had a profound impact on how students saw themselves and their attachment to the larger social world was Mildred Pitts Walter's *Darkness*. The author gives examples of positive events that happen in the dark and why darkness should not be feared. We connected this concept to the larger world and how fear can be debilitating in accomplishing goals and making changes at a personal and greater level. Each of these books, which were the curricula, helped students to make meaningful connections to larger social worlds.

Powerful Examples

As previously discussed, students bring valuable perspectives and experiences to texts. A multicultural reading of a text can occur when students are encouraged to question inferred messages and how they promote or challenge stereotypes. This is precisely what happened as Jodene's fourth graders read *Oh, California*, the California history textbook. After reading about the completion of the transcontinental railroad and the laborers, primarily Irish immigrants and Chinese immigrants who were part of the "Coolie" slave trade, we studied a photograph taken at Promontory Point, Utah. One of the students asked, "Why's everyone white?" While the textbook discussed the workers from various backgrounds, it failed to provide a critique of the photograph and why the laborers were absent. In response, the students sought outside sources such as Zinn's *A People's History of the United States* to learn more about the railroad and immigration. Through our analytic discussions, they learned about the importance of diversity and giving voice to all participants.

As a literacy specialist, Jodene worked closely with elementary and middle-school teachers. Similar to the previous example of how students bring a multicultural perspective to texts, sixth-grade students drew on their understanding of racism and issues of power and were extremely upset while reading the original print version of Taylor's *The Cay* from 1969 and listening to an abridged audio recording from 1992. They discovered that the audio recording omitted blatantly racist language, which was critical to understanding the main characters' relationship transformation. Timothy, a Black West Indian man, addresses Phillip, a white American boy, as "young bahss" or "bahss" throughout the beginning of the written narrative but this is omitted fifty-eight times in the audio-recording. Without the repeated use of the term, readers are not reminded to continually consider the socially constructed racialized roles of the characters. The students immediately recognized and questioned the omission of the term as well as offensive, racist language found in the written text. While *The Cay* is not typically labeled as multicultural, it is saturated with inferred messages about race, power, and positionality. The students brought a multicultural read to the text and with the support and encouragement of their teacher, questioned possible reasons for the omissions and racial sterilization. Teaching students to do this across all genres of texts is both empowering and instrumental in making connections.

In the previous examples, upper elementary students brought multicultural perspectives to their readings of literary texts. The next example illustrates why this is equally important and possible with younger children. While supervising a student teacher in a Kindergarten class, Jodene observed how students made personal connections to a biography of Abraham Lincoln and how a multicultural read was both hampered and encouraged by the student teacher. After reading the biography, the apprenticing teacher asked students to share key information about Lincoln's life. The first two students shared that Lincoln was president and wanted everyone to be free, which addressed inequality in society and racism, albeit at a superficial level. The teacher called on the third child who shared that Lincoln's mother died when he was very young. Rather than adding the child's comment to the flip chart with the first two comments, the teacher told the child that they should "keep it happy." The child did not raise his hand again. When I asked the student teacher why she wanted to "keep it happy," she replied that the child's aunt was dying of cancer. Once she shared this fact, she realized her error in not validating his response to help him make a meaningful personal connection to the text and the message it sent to the other children. We then discussed why it was important for the students to see themselves in the texts. While only 3 percent of the students in the school identified as white, similar to Lincoln, and came from diverse cultural backgrounds, they were looking for connections to their own lives and focusing on information that had personal meaning. Invalidating the child's response compromised his attachment to the text, the student teacher, and his learning environment.

By encouraging students to bring a multicultural read to texts, teachers can help students find attachment to the texts, adults, and students in the classroom. This type of teaching and learning can successfully occur across grades and content areas. The previous examples are just a handful of ways in which teachers can validate or invalidate students' lived experiences and perspectives. While we strongly encourage the use of authentic and accurate multicultural literature across K-12, we also believe that any text can be read from a multicultural perspective to challenge and embrace inferred messages.

Ernest regularly works with high-school English teachers to develop curricula that are culturally sustaining and academically rigorous. Part of this work involves a collaborative inquiry process where teachers are asking difficult questions about practice and designing and investigating innovative classroom approaches. One of the teachers who has been involved in this work for some time was teaching *Bless Me, Ultima* to a ninth-grade class. The novel's protagonist is a young boy, Antonio, who is coming to terms with numerous dual identities. At once he is caught between the worlds of Mexico and America, the languages of Spanish and English, the city and the country, the religions of Europeans and Native Americans, and, finally he is somewhere between the worlds of childhood and adulthood. In the story the protagonist's family is visited by Ultima, a curandera (a healer) who helps him to reconcile many of these competing influences. In short, the curandera helps the main character to embrace his multicultural identity as he prepares to make difficult choices about his future.

The class where *Bless Me, Ultima* was being taught had many students who were facing similar challenges. Not only were they the same age, but many were also migrants or from a family that had recently migrated either to the city, to the West Coast, or to the United States. All of the students had competing cultural influences that they would have to reconcile in forming their identities as students and as members of families and communities. In designing a curriculum that would be relevant to her class, the teacher and I decided that it would be interesting to have the students in class perform oral histories of their elders, learning from them about their experiences of (im)migration and their commentary on issues such as schooling, education, and cultural transmission. We worked with the students to develop a protocol that they would use to interview these elders (everyone had two interviews to conduct). The students then transcribed key elements of the interviews that would be used for their final essays. The students also created PowerPoint presentations that included background information on the interviewees, a synopsis of the responses to the questions, and the sharing of a family artifact. All of the students included pictures of the elders they interviewed. The final stage included a public presentation of the PowerPoint slides, which they did in class and also as guests at a local university. The use of the oral history assignment exposed the students to elements of their own family history that many of them did not know. It also allowed for the family members and other elders to contribute to the knowledge production of the classroom. Finally, the students were able to better identify with the protagonist and with the themes of the story.

Literature Pedagogy for Today's Classrooms

There is no question that America's classrooms are becoming more diverse places and there is also little question that the world of the twenty-first century will require future generations to not only "tolerate" this diversity, but to embrace it as an asset that makes communities stronger and our collective experience on the planet better as we learn from and draw from one another's strengths. In our estimation this sort of education has to begin very early and there is no better way to develop this critical literacy and social awareness than through empowering multicultural readings of multicultural literatures. We also know that nurturing attachments with peers and teachers, as well as the academic, literary, and larger social world can happen for students of all ages when they are taught and encouraged to engage in multicultural reading. Ideally, through this type of learning and reading, students will develop mutual recognition of and appreciation for one another inside the classroom and toward others beyond the classroom.

CHAPTER THREE

Linking the Word to the World: Connecting Multicultural Children's Literature to the Lives of Twenty-first Century Youth

Students just returned from recess and are settling in at their desks, on the couch at the back of the room, or on the floor with legs stretched out as their fifth-grade teacher grabs his copy of Pam Munoz-Ryan's Echo from his desk and continues reading aloud from where they left off the day before. Written in three parts and framed in the beginning and end by a fairy tale, the novel is primarily set a few years prior and after the Second World War which aligns with their grade level Social Studies curriculum—US History. The class is starting to work on small group projects for their unit, Unsung American Heroes of World War II, that bridge Social Studies and ELA. The week before, several students expressed excitement about graphic novels, so for their project, the teacher encouraged them to use a graphic novel as one of their sources. One group chose George Takei's "They Called Us Enemy" about Japanese American Internment camps and another chose Blake Hoana's "Navajo Code Talkers Top Secret Messengers of World War II." They will be creating multimedia projects that include various sources such as videos, books, interviews, artwork, and literature. Both groups have decided to create their own short graphic novels as part of their final project. Another group is interested in the Tuskegee Airmen but can only find a book intended for younger readers in the "Who Was" series called "Who Were the Tuskegee Airmen." They are planning to write, perform, and videotape a skit to go along with the book for younger grades in their school. With these projects, students are learning about various genres and forms (Echo: historical fiction and fantasy; They Called Us Enemy: graphic novel and memoir; Navajo Code Talkers: graphic novel and informational text; Who Were the Tuskegee Airmen: biography), honoring and sharing the story of groups often left out of history books, and creating projects to share with a wide audience. The projects are multimedia, literature based, and intended to serve as counternarratives to traditional texts about the Second World War that downplay the contributions of racially oppressed groups. The teacher is recalling an article he read in college, Nancy Larrick's "The All White World of Children's Literature" and appreciates the enthusiasm of his students, who do not reflect the African Americans, Native Americans, or Japanese Americans in their chosen texts, but who aim to tell a more complete story of all Americans' contributions.

The idea of linking the world of the classroom to the worlds of our students is nothing new in education. More than a 100 years ago educational pioneer John Dewey (1901) highlighted the importance of centering learning in the worlds of children. Throughout the twentieth century critical scholars such as Paulo Freire and Gloria Ladson-Billings encouraged educators to embed classroom practices in the everyday experiences of students (Freire, 1970) and to create lessons that increased cultural competence among historically marginalized students (Ladson-Billings, 1994). When we are able to use multicultural children's literature to link the world of the classroom to the lives of students, we increase motivation, engagement, achievement, and relevance and we promote active learning that stimulates curiosity, creativity, and the social awareness needed to foster kindness, courage, and hope (Allyn & Morrell, 2016).

However, it isn't always so easy to translate these ideas into practice in the multi-faceted America of the twenty-first century. A world filled with languages and cultures and constantly changing demographics in our schools, but also a world filled with new technologies, new ways of acquiring and transmitting language that have radically changed the way we live. While it may seem intuitive to us in our everyday lives that the world is rapidly changing, we must also acknowledge that English Language Arts can often be resistant to these changes. We recognize that some teachers may feel pressure to strictly adhere to a particular curriculum or focus on test preparation for high stakes tests, which may not allow time and space for supplemental texts that accurately and authentically reflect their students' experiences and identities. These factors present a tension between our ideas and our instincts and the mandates and standards that we live and work within.

In this chapter, we play out some of these contradictions and tensions as they relate to the teaching of multicultural literature as we play out what it has meant for us in our sixty collective years of teaching and working with K-12 literacy teachers across the country in large districts with diverse student populations, to link the teaching of literature to the worlds of our students. We talk about what this means in terms of the selection of the texts that we teach, the theory of reading that we promote, the writing we ask students to do, and finally how we link the lessons learned inside of the classroom to action in the world around us.

How We Choose the Texts We Read

We need a broader array of stories in our classrooms because children need to see themselves in the stories they read (Bishop, 1990; Morrell & Morrell, 2012). As Henry Louis Gates mentions in his introduction to *The Classic Slave Narratives*, true literacy for historically marginalized groups entails the ability to write ourselves into being (Gates, 2002). Through the stories we share we affirm ourselves and our existence as unique and varied as our existences may be. So, when we say that children need to see themselves in the stories that they read we mean that literally and figuratively. In a diverse selection, students will see others who come from similar frames of reference including but not limited to culture, geography, and ethnicity. But students should be able to identify across these simple markers to see those with whom they would have other affinities, interests, and concerns about the world. We would hate to suggest that students should not only be able to relate to texts where the authors come from a similar cultural or geographical background. Students should be encouraged to relate to authors and texts of all sorts. However, it would beg the question if students never saw themselves literally in the texts that they read. Ebony Elizabeth Thomas (2016), notable scholar of children's and young adult literature, asserts that we need "more accurate and humanizing representations of children of color" (p. 113) and that "stories still matter, and always will" (p. 118). Fortunately, with the growing selection of multicultural texts across the K-12 spectrum, more children are seeing themselves in positive and authentic ways in literature.

Choice of texts can happen in a variety of ways. There are the texts that the whole class reads and discusses, such as read alouds, and these should be varied in background and perspective. We often think of read alouds as only appropriate for elementary students; however, read alouds can be used with older students to introduce a new concept, encourage and scaffold dialogue, and develop a deeper interest in reading. Teachers and older students can select texts that are age- and developmentally appropriate but that students might not be able to read independently due to the difficulty of the text or texts that can be better understood with whole and small group discussion (Allington, 2001). As Colabucci, Napoli, Ward, and Day (2016) suggest, read alouds should play an integral role in literacy classrooms to engage and motivate readers while "supporting vocabulary development, critical thinking, and listening comprehension" (p. 49). This is especially true for classes with a significant number of students for whom English is a new language or students reading below grade level. In elementary classrooms, teachers and students can select trade books that are appropriate for guided reading groups which feature interesting and engaging topics (e.g., non-fiction) and plots and characters (fiction). As mentioned, the range of well-written and interesting multicultural books from easy to advanced levels is broad and continually growing. Recently, books by and about individuals of color, including authors such as Meg Medina, Veera Hiranandani, Erin Entrada Kelly, Derrick Barnes, Jason Reynolds, Kwame Alexander, and Renee Watson have received notable attention and various awards by the American Library Association, which is evidence of the increasing stature of multicultural literature. And according to statistics compiled by the Cooperative Children's Book Center (CCBC), the number of books by and about African/ African Americans, Asian Pacific and Asian Pacific Americans, and Latinx continues to grow at a promising and steady rate (Cooperative Children's Book Center, 2022).

There are also texts that students read on their own. This is where we have tremendous flexibility in choosing texts that are highly motivating and engaging. In his work with middle-school students Jeff Wilhelm (2016) found greater success when he allowed his struggling boys to select texts that had meaning for them. When working with upper elementary boys, Jodene has found that the most popular books are biographies of athletes and celebrities, classic and contemporary comic books, graphic novels, books related to movies and video games, and non-fiction. When these books are available in the classroom and school library, students can look forward to independent reading time because they have choices and the books have meaning for them.

To engage and motivate students to read, they must see connections between their lives and the texts. They need to imagine and see themselves in the texts that are used throughout the day and across the curriculum. Fortunately, we have a tremendous selection of books that address themes such as social justice, community, and collaboration and non-fiction on topics that are interesting and relevant to students. These can be incorporated into and supplement the required curriculum to support and extend students' learning while strategically meeting their specific reading needs and interests.

How We Read the Texts We Choose

Simply stated, "Reading is not a monolithic activity" (Paulson & Armstrong, 2010, p. 8). Readers bring a tremendous range of background knowledge, interests, and perspectives to texts that can be as varied as novels, poetry, grocery lists, traffic signs, and newspapers, to name a few. In the classroom, students express varying degrees of motivation and interest in reading depending on the text. And we should no longer assume that their reading stance fits neatly on a traditional continuum with an efferent stance at one end and aesthetic stance at the other (Paulson & Armstrong, 2010). Reading is a complex process depending on the reader and the text; therefore, we propose a new theory of reading which draws on existing research while focusing on how we connect literature for children to the lives of our students. Reading is not solely about decoding words; rather, students should be actively reading to make meaningful connections, enhancing their understanding of the world, and increasing their empathy and authentic care of others. In Paulo Freire's words,

Reading does not consist merely of decoding the written word or language; rather, it is preceded by and intertwined with knowledge of the world. Language and reality are dynamically interconnected. The understanding attained by critical reading of a text implies perceiving the relationship between text and context.

(1987, p. 19)

Obviously readers need to learn phonics, phonemic awareness, fluency, and text reading comprehension skills to become fluent readers (Snow, Griffin & Burns, 2005), but this is just the starting point. We need to ask ourselves several questions about how we teach our students *how* to read. How do our students use what they have read to truly transform their ideas and views of the world? How do they connect with texts and grow as a reader and citizen? How can they draw on the texts to improve their writing? These are just some of the questions we believe our theory of reading addresses.

We strongly believe multicultural literature should be included in the curriculum across grade levels and content areas. Because our student population is rapidly changing nationally, with our schools already more than 54 percent non-white (NCES, 2022), we need to provide texts that reflect this racial, ethnic, and cultural diversity. While students can make text-to-self connections with any text, we feel it is extremely important for students to see themselves (i.e., culturally, geographically, socioeconomically, etc.) in obvious and blatant ways in the words and illustrations they encounter. However, when students do not see themselves specifically in terms of culture, ethnicity, geography, etc., in the texts, we believe they should be taught to read from a multicultural perspective. By this we mean that students bring multiple cultural and critical perspectives to any texts they read and we need to teach them how to tap into these perspectives.

When Jodene was working as a middle-school literacy specialist in the midwest, she collaborated with a fifth-grade teacher as the class read Christopher Paul Curtis's *Watsons*

Go to Birmingham—1963. Half of the twenty students had come to the school through international refugee services and as a whole, the twenty students represented ten birth countries and collectively spoke ten different home languages (English, Somali, Spanish, Vietnamese, Arabic, Kurdish, Haitian-Creole, Dinka, and Swahili). Their time in the United States ranged from 1.5 to 13 years. It was impossible to find a text that represented all of their home cultures and unique and diverse experiences; therefore, while reading the novel we guided students in taking up the perspectives of the characters, especially Kenny, an African American child living in Flint, Michigan, in 1963. Our students became invested in the Watson family and discovered ways to create deep connections to the characters and imagine how life may have been during this time period. They laughed at Kenny's misunderstandings and his brother's antics, loved Kenny's sweet little sister, and felt like a member of the family. As the Watsons traveled to the South and experienced a horrific event, our students were visibly upset and expressed tremendous grief and anger during our discussions and in their writing. While the majority of students did not share the same ethnic, cultural, or socioeconomic background as the Watsons, they did deepen their knowledge of the 1960s and most importantly expressed empathy and authentic emotions throughout their reading of the novel.

Students should continue to make a range of connections (text-to-self, text-to-text, and text-to-world) to not only increase their comprehension of the specific text, but to take what they read and apply it in meaningful ways. By making these types of connections, they are more motivated, engaged, and empowered as readers. Since we want reading to be authentic and for students to see a clear purpose, whether this is to learn about the world and themselves or for the sheer joy of learning, it is important to provide them with a wide range of literature that promotes tolerance and acceptance and challenges stereotypes and essentializing. High-quality multicultural literature can serve this purpose to not only help in the teaching of reading, but also to develop students' understanding of social community action and their role as active and informed citizens.

Finally, when we think about how we want our students to read we should also be thinking about how we want them to write. When students have opportunities to engage in thought-provoking, personal and intellectual discussions about their readings, these ideas and perspectives make their way into the students' writing. In the next section, we consider how students use their multicultural readings as a springboard to rewrite the world.

Re-writing the World: Telling Our Stories as a Response to Multicultural Literature

The changing landscape of K-12 education is requiring more writing from students across the disciplines and grade levels. Where literacy in our field was once synonymous with "reading" we now understand that students must leave our classrooms with an ability to express their thoughts and feelings through writing in multiple genres and for multiple audiences. We feel that this is a positive change, for writing represents voice and one of the most powerful and lasting effects of a critical education is to instill students with the consciousness, the confidence, and the literacy tools to be compassionate and outspoken advocates for the people and purposes they care about. Even further we know that the creative industries, the landscape of social entrepreneurialism, and the businesses of disruptive technologies require those who have a command of the written word. We believe that a curriculum that foregrounds multicultural literature can inspire this kind of writing.

One of the historical reasons that people have written their stories down is to commemorate important migrations and transitions in their lives and the lives of people they care about. In this way, Gloria Anzaldua (1987) argues, we learn more about ourselves and our values through the stories that we tell ourselves about ourselves as we navigate the borders of multiple cultures and ways of being in the world. Telling and retelling our stories facilitates memory, presence, perseverance, and consciousness. This is certainly important for our students who are often asked to navigate multiple cultural borders defined by ethnicity, language, religion, age, geography, and socioeconomic status. To facilitate the writing of their own stories, there are many books across the K-8 spectrum that deal with migrations and transitions into new worlds. Whether it is the first day of school (*Chocolate Milk, Por Favor; I'm New Here; The Name Jar*) a move to a new city, or moving to a new country where very few people speak your language (*Dreamers; Lucky Broken Girl; One Green Apple; Front Desk*) these transitions can be very traumatic for children and their families. Literacy teachers can use these narratives as an opportunity to allow students to share their own stories of migration and transition. Students can also learn to empathize with others who are experiencing these sorts of transitions. As examples on the upper end of this spectrum, Ernest has worked with teachers who have used stories like Kwame Alexander's *The Crossover* and Matt de la Peña's *Ball Don't Lie* to encourage students to tell stories about their lives, their families and their communities in verse and prose. As a final example, we all know of stories that point to harmful conditions in our cities and in the larger society. These stories deal with bullying (*The Curse of the Bully's Wrath/La Maldición De La Ira Del Abusón; Tales from the Bully Box; Lucky Luna*), harm to the environment, or ethnic or religious intolerance (*Nasreen's Secret School*). We know of many examples of teachers whose students have wanted to engage in social action based upon their readings of texts. The writing can take the form of letters to school and public officials, newsletters and pamphlets on environmental awareness, or even drama, as Ernest witnessed while working with a third-grade teacher whose class created a forum-theater play pointing to the economic and structural causes underlying neighborhood violence after reading children's literature that discussed violence in cities. Engaging literature has the power to motivate students to write and since the most effective way to improve writing is through reading, we owe it to our students to provide a variety of texts to which they connect in multifaceted ways.

One example of how a third-grade teacher came to use literature to transform her classroom culture began when she told Jodene how upset she felt by the way her children were interacting with one another at the start of the school year. The children were quick to anger, push each other, and speak without kindness or empathy toward one another. The teacher was also concerned about her literacy instruction and how to increase the amount of writing throughout the day. In an attempt to improve the classroom culture and increase writing production, we found several picture books about friendship and bullying (e.g., *Nobody Knew What to Do; My Secret Bully; Sorry*) to use as read alouds each week, to engage students in thoughtful discussions about how they could connect to the characters and situations in the book, and how they might be kinder to one another to create a safer and more compassionate learning environment. By the middle of the school year, students had filled their writing journals with reflections about the read alouds which improved not only their comprehension, but also their writing production and small group discussions. They became so passionate about improving their community that they began an anti-bullying movement at their school by talking with other students and posting anti-bullying signs and posters with positive messages in the hallways. By the end of the school year, the teacher was so inspired by the kindness her students were expressing to one another that she continued to use the same books the following year to teach empathy and kindness, to motivate her students to write, and to impact their school culture in concrete and powerful ways.

While we should be encouraging our students to read and write beyond the regular school day, as elementary educators our focus should be on explicit, excellent writing instruction across genres throughout the school day and for middle and secondary educators, explicit and excellent writing instruction in discipline. Literature can provide templates or models across genres and offer engaging and thought-provoking multicultural perspectives to motivate students to read and write. For example, there are thousands of versions of Cinderella throughout the world (e.g., *Murafo's Beautiful Daughters, The Rough Faced Girl, Adelita, Yeh-Shen*) representing a rich diversity of cultures and perspectives. When teaching fairy tales and folktales, teachers can select versions of Cinderella to show how writers begin with a premise and add their own cultural perspectives and details. When teaching writing in middle school, Jodene used selected vignettes from Sandra Cisneros's *The House on Mango Street* to teach students to write vignettes. Many of the sixth- and seventh-grade boys and girls who claimed to dislike reading and writing found copies of books, such as Sharon Flake's *The Skin I'm In* and Walter Dean Myers' *Monster,* to read the entire texts on their own after hearing the first half of the books as read alouds. We often think of narratives as models, but we can also use texts by great expository writers to see how the authors use voice and creative techniques (Duke, 2010).

Inspiring writing through a rich and diverse selection of literature can be one way to motivate students—even students who claim to dislike writing and do not see themselves as writers. Providing constructive, specific feedback and abundant opportunities to write will also increase the amount and improve the quality of the texts students produce. By combining reading and writing throughout the day or a class period, students will see the close connection between the two and how reading can both inspire and improve their ability to rewrite the world.

Connecting Themes of Literature to the Social World and Community Action

One strategy for engaging students via literature is to draw upon the themes and issues brought up in these texts to develop social action projects that students can undertake in their own neighborhoods and communities. Working within the Youth Participatory Action Research tradition (YPAR) (Mirra, Garcia & Morrell, 2016) we regularly ask students how they would like to change the world. Great literature should encourage us to think and act differently so we recommend that final projects push students out into the real world as much as possible.

For twelve years, Ernest directed a YPAR project out of UCLA where students attending Los Angeles schools developed social action projects based on issues that mattered to them. Teachers would assign students multicultural literature to inspire discussion and reflection on their lives and the world around them. Subsequently these teachers would take the students through a ten-step project that asked students to:

1 Identify a Problem

2 Develop a Question

3 Design a Study

4 Collect Data

5 Analyze Data

6 Produce Claims

7 Provide Evidence

8 Create Products

9 Disseminate Products

10 Take Social Action

In one example, Ernest assigned students Langston Hughes's "Dream Deferred" poem and asked them to consider how the lost dreams of youth might inspire research and social action projects. Students chose to study the media and its impact on youth trajectories, curriculum offerings in K-12 schools, how economic downturns influenced opportunities in communities, and access to books and learning materials in communities to name a few. Each group developed a research report, a video documentary, and a virtual presentation to share with community members, the local media, and local and state politicians including the mayor, the district superintendent, and several state senators. Ernest and his research team analyzed the student reports for evidence of academic and critical literacies and they tracked student participants in the program to see whether YPAR had any impact on their likelihood to take advanced courses, to graduate high school, and to enroll in and persist through college (Mirra, Garcia & Morrell, 2016).

In another example of how literature inspires community action, a fourth-grade class in California read children's books depicting the civil rights movement as part of a larger unit on education and justice. These students then began to study the conditions in their own schools in comparison to schools in surrounding neighborhoods to see if education had changed very much in the fifty years since Marshall had fought against school segregation in the *Brown v. Board of Education* Supreme Court case. The students interviewed their peers and they examined reports on school achievement. They also used the Internet to look up other schools in more affluent communities. Ultimately, the students shared their research report via a PowerPoint presentation and a Theater of the Oppressed-style play that they wrote themselves to audiences of educators and pre-service teachers. They also wrote letters to their local superintendent sharing the findings of their research and offering recommendations for how to promote equity in their school system.

Fostering a Love of Literature and Student Voice

While we struggle to find ways to promote excellence and achievement in literacy for all of our students, we remain steadfast in our belief that all students want to learn and do well. We also believe that most students possess the intellectual capability to become powerful readers and writers in our classrooms. Tapping into students' background knowledge and experiences, connecting great multicultural literature to the everyday lives of students, and allowing students to use their experiences with literature to speak to issues they care about will increase the confidence and the motivation that our students need to succeed in school. Even further, we believe that these approaches will foster a love of literature and of voice via the written word.

We agree with Patrick Shannon (2016) that the idea of reading for pleasure might be found in the past as suggested by progressive educators such as John Dewey and Francis Parker, particularly with a learner-centered approach and a belief that "learning is natural, challenging and enjoyable and students are interested and interesting" (p. 39). We take up these ideas and suggest that offering students choice and a wide range of multicultural literature across all grades and content areas will help them to develop empathy, celebrate their own experiences and interests, and inspire them to write and read for authentic purposes. We have offered examples of how teachers have used literature across K-12 classrooms as the foundation for their writing units while building students' love of literature and often leading to social action. With the consistent increase and availability of high-quality multicultural literature and resources to assist with selecting literature, such as the Notable Books for a Global Society: Empathy, Caring and Understanding from Multiple Perspectives, which dates back to 2016 and provides annual lists of suggested books, we are optimistic that teachers can draw on our suggestions to foster a love of literature with their students while helping students to become more powerful readers and writers.

CHAPTER FOUR

Student Voice and Agency in the Polyvocal Literature Classroom

A sixth-grade middle school English Language Arts teacher is using literature to teach her students about the importance of voice in writing. She wants to create more opportunities in her class for small group discussion to encourage all students to participate. Her students love to listen to read alouds so she begins the unit on Voice with an interactive read aloud of the classic 1944 Newbery Honor book The Hundred Dresses by Eleanor Estes. The story is based on Estes' childhood experience of being a bystander when Wanda Petronski, a child in her small town class in Connecticut, is mocked for her Polish accent and owning only one tattered dress, which she cleans and wears daily. Wanda moves away and the protagonist, Maddie, is never able to apologize for her silence. The teacher reads the short novel in two days, stopping periodically to provide historical and cultural context and to engage the students in whole class discussion. They discuss Estes' use of voice, or lack of, by the protagonist—capturing the distress, regret, and frustration of a child in convincing ways through her self-talk and dialogue with others. The class then chooses to read either "Harbor Me" or "Brown Girl

Dreaming" (both by Jacqueline Woodson) for their literature study. She then divides the two groups (two per novel) once more for a total of four groups which become their "expert groups." She has intentionally grouped the students based on their personalities and ways of participating in small groups. The more boisterous, outgoing, and high-energy students are grouped together and the quiet, more reserved students are grouped together to avoid a single or small group of children from dominating the discussion. The expert groups are creating posters of their novels—including specific examples of voice, commentary, and visual representations of how the author focuses on voice. They practice talking about their poster. They will then be the "expert" and talk about their poster with students from the other groups (one student from each group becomes the "teaching group").

Why Student Voice Matters

It was early in the fall of 1993, Ernest's first year teaching full-time at East Bay High School in Northern California. His students were moving about the classroom excitedly as they were working in groups on an assignment, the writing of one-act plays that dealt with contemporary issues. The hum of classroom engagement was disrupted by a pounding on the classroom door. In the doorframe stood the imposing figure of one of the veteran teachers in the school, who happened to occupy the classroom directly below. "Where is your teacher?!" the voice bellowed as the students froze in silence. Ernest replied, just as terrified as his students, "I'm right here. The students are just working on a group assignment." The teacher flashed a smile. "Oh, I heard the noise and I thought you were gone ..." The veteran and the rookie teacher shared a good laugh before she headed back downstairs.

Even as we began our careers almost thirty years ago, a quiet classroom was considered a well-managed classroom. As an early-career teacher, Ernest found himself having to convince students, colleagues, and administrators that the noise in his classroom was both intentional and good! We contend that humans are social beings and learn through social interactions and oral communication. In this chapter, we use the term "polyvocal" to mean multiple voices and assert that in a classroom, every voice deserves respect and each student should be embraced as a valuable contributor. Many of these early ideas were inspired by our readings of Paulo Freire as young teachers. The idea of teachers and students engaging in authentic dialogue, or even of the classroom being filled with animated voices of students were foreign to our city schools in the early 1990s. Still the idea of true authentic dialogue stuck as we matured in our understanding of Paulo Freire and the possibilities for polyvocal classrooms. When teachers and students truly listen to one another, each person is told their voice matters. From a practical perspective, how can we know our students' thoughts if they do not orally articulate their ideas, receive critical feedback, and revise or solidify their thoughts? Creating a classroom culture where every voice is honored nurtures learning as much as it encourages students to share their ideas to grow as learners and community members. For the remainder of this chapter, we will discuss student voice as responsive pedagogy with a focus on whole class and small group discussions, multimodal presentations, and student-initiated research. Each section includes examples from classroom practice.

Student Voice as the Ultimate in Responsive Pedagogy

There is much talk these days about culturally responsive pedagogy and for good reason. As our classrooms become more diverse and as the world gets smaller, our need to honor and leverage multiculturalism becomes our greatest strength. Yet finding the right balance presents itself as a challenge when culturally responsive pedagogy becomes a game of matching faces on books to faces in the classroom. How much of one group should students have access to in a completely homogeneous classroom? How much should we oversample when our classrooms are less diverse, but filled with students from nondominant backgrounds? What should the mix look like when the students are almost exclusively from a dominant culture? And how do we teach the texts we choose? Does that matter?

Of course, it all matters. But a curriculum that is just focused on who gets taught may never necessarily become culturally responsive. We work from a three-part framework to conceptualize the culturally responsive classroom: (1) re-presentation, (2) intercultural understanding, and (3) student voice. By all means we want a dynamic mix of dominant and nondominant voices in all classrooms and we want diverse texts in terms of period, genre, gender, race, and perspective re-presented to students in a way that gives them some significant ownership over their readings of these texts. Elsewhere (Morrell & Morrell, 2012; Morrell & Morrell, 2021) we argue for multicultural readings of texts that are led by critical questioning. A re-presentation of ALL texts can make them available for multicultural and critical interpretation. Second, a culturally responsive classroom should provide spaces for dialogue and engagement that increase intercultural understanding. Not only do we see ourselves differently, but we learn to better situate ourselves within a larger network of humanity; hopefully in greater love and respect for that larger human family.

However, for us, the most important component of a responsive curriculum is honoring and leveraging student voice. A responsive classroom should be defined not by what we give to students but by how we make it possible for them to say and do. Unencumbered voice is, by definition, responsive. Students tell us what they think, what they want, and how they want to be impactful upon the world. Student voice manifests in all sorts of ways, from allowing students to choose the books they read independently, creating spaces for community-action projects at the end of literary units, to polyvocal modalities of communication in the classroom. It is this last component that we focus on in this chapter. In doing so, we place the polyvocal classroom at the center of a model of instruction that can be culturally responsive for all students at all times.

The Power of the Polyvocal Classroom

The majority of our waking hours are spent communicating, whether it is listening, speaking, reading, or writing. Through these discourse genres, students develop identities; gain an awareness of others' perspectives; and, ultimately, they become better members of families, communities, and the public sphere. Scholars as diverse as Jürgen Habermas, John Dewey, and Paulo Freire have spoken to the importance of dialogue to the development of fully realized humans and a vibrant democracy. Even still, speaking and listening are seldom highlighted in contemporary literacy classrooms. We consider here how they can become more central to the work of responsive literacy instruction. We use the term "polyvocal classroom" to mean a place where many different interlocutors are able to share their voices powerfully and listen thoughtfully to the voices of others.

The benefits of classroom talk are immense and contribute to academic gains, such as improved writing, and social-emotional growth such as engagement and confidence. Classroom talk is also a means to develop a generative and caring community, which is essential for students' academic and social-emotional growth.

Classroom talk is critical to healthy community development. When students have opportunities to talk with one another they share beyond bits of discrete information to share about themselves and see one another as whole, complex individuals. Communities often have shared values and beliefs and this requires time and space for candid consistent dialogue.

Relationships are not built by being in the same space; rather, genuine interactions and conversations allow members to identify mutual interests and in this case, work toward common goals. We should also consider the importance of community in terms of belonging, one of the seven strengths discussed in Allyn and Morrell's (2016) book *Every Child a Super Reader*. They state, "For a child to flourish, she must know that she is a valued member of a community and that her unique voice is respected" (p. 32). The authors focus on younger students, but the theory applies to older students and adults. When a student is a valued member of a community, they are invested and engaged because their ideas are taken seriously and their contributions matter. With opportunities to discuss their ideas with peers, their oral language improves. This is clearly evident for students learning English. They can listen to their peers modeling oral language, likely in multiple registers, which allows them to develop both conversational and academic English.

Classroom talk facilitates better writing. A high-school English teacher in Los Angeles shared with pre-service teachers how she required students to talk through their papers with two different peers before writing. The process forced them to formulate and fine-tune their ideas, field questions from their partners, and consider elements that were missing or weak. She noticed significant improvement in students' rough drafts, which made revising and editing less overwhelming and produced clear and concise writing. A high-school history teacher in Northern California had his students compose papers together, initially because of the overwhelming number of students in each class. He quickly discovered that by talking through their ideas and working together, they produced superior writing compared to when they worked alone without discussing ideas with peers. Through this process, they taught one another, learned together, and composed stronger papers.

Low stakes opportunities for classroom talk allows students to develop public speaking skills. When they orally share ideas with a few other students, they develop confidence. Students in the role of audience hone their listening skills so they can engage others in thoughtful conversation and offer constructive feedback. We can see the benefits of practicing public speaking as it moves from small groups to large groups in our everyday practice. Allowing students to talk to just one other person or a small group and then return to the whole group produces richer conversation as they try out ideas and build confidence.

The remainder of this chapter focuses on four activity systems that are powerful generators of student voice: the whole class discussion, the small group discussion, the classroom debate, and formal presentations. Ernest honed in on these areas while working with schools in the Mid-Atlantic States throughout the 2010s. One of the schools identified student voice and agency as the area they wanted to improve the most. Ernest, along with the English department teachers identified these four classroom activities as the most promising to drill into. They created frameworks for measuring student participation and learning, they shared exemplary practice within these activity settings, and they shared these understandings in a professional learning community that met weekly to discuss innovative pedagogical approaches. It is no surprise that one of these schools, led by first-year co-Principals, became one of the top five turnaround schools in the state. Needless to say, Ernest became hooked on the power of polyvocal English classrooms improving student voice, student agency, and student achievement.

Whole Class Discussions

Whole-class teacher-led student-centered discussions should remain the hallmark of the polyvocal classroom. During whole class discussions, the teacher models the confident, yet reflective interlocutor while also allowing for students to develop their critical thinking, speaking, and listening skills. Specifically, we help students learn how to think out loud and how to share ideas that are still baking in the oven to solicit feedback and refinement. We also provide scripts, specific language, for how to clarify and synthesize ideas and how to disagree by acknowledging differing points of view in a respectful way. We suggest working on these scripts with the class and posting the agreed upon language in the class as an anchor chart.

With the support of the teacher, students develop as active participants with critical communication skills that are essential to life in a polyvocal classroom. First among these are critical listening skills since students spend 95 percent of the time listening in the whole class discussion. They also become better questioners and more thoughtful participants who understand how to take appropriate turns by jumping into and out of conversations. In a well-running whole class discussion, students will take multiple turns building from each other's arguments while the teacher will facilitate with an occasional interjection. Students will also learn to reflect on their own participation in whole class discussions and they will develop a sense of the skill sets they need to develop. We suggest having spaces at the end of units for students to reflect on their own learning and participation; this would include asking them to evaluate their participation in whole group discussions. Over the course of the year we would expect them to acknowledge and address areas that need improvement (e.g., soliciting feedback, addressing others in the classroom by name, leaning in as a listener, making points succinctly, and being willing to introduce unpopular arguments).

Small Group Discussions

We find that the biggest variable in classrooms is the amount of time spent in small group discussion. Powerful polyvocal classrooms set aside a substantive proportion for these small group encounters. They provide an opportunity for more students to speak, they allow the teacher time to work with a smaller number of students, they increase student agency, and they allow students to get to know one another more intimately in larger classroom settings. Often small groups are abandoned because students may have not been taught how to properly thrive in these environments. We consider the abandonment of small group discussion time as a significant opportunity loss for powerful learning. We believe there needs to be more of a focus in English classrooms on how to make the skills and sensibilities that maximize this student-led, student-centered space more transparent.

In a small group discussion, students should understand how to get in formation, similar to a huddle in sports. The formation is important, because it signifies that the group is cohesive, intimate, and focused on collectively producing knowledge. The formation also connotes that unnecessary items be removed from the circle or cluster, and that students lean into one another so that they can better listen and communicate. Some classrooms are already structured in table groups and these may be fine, but the cluster of chairs or even having students seated on the floor or standing can make for better cohesion. They also reduce the noise in the classroom so that other groups are not disturbed or distracted.

There are two ways we form small groups. One assigns a group leader who will facilitate the conversation and the other allows for co-facilitation, where all students are responsible for maintaining the culture of the group. Whether sole-facilitating or co-facilitating, it is our responsibility to help students learn how to be responsible for each other in small groups. We should talk to them about strategies for how to pull someone into the conversation if they're on the outskirts. We should discuss as a class how to politely push someone back if they're dominating the conversation, how to bring synthesis or how to agree to disagree (it is important that they come to understand the value of productive tensions). Over the course of a school year, we can help students to develop a collective aesthetic of small group life, we can help them to develop the skills they need to be effective interlocutors in small groups, and we can provide spaces for them to reflect on their participation in small groups while identifying their strengths and areas for growth.

One way to model a respectful and productive small group discussion is with a "fish bowl." A small group of student volunteers create a circle of chairs in the center of the room and the rest of the students create a concentric circle. The small group is given a topic that everyone can speak about and they discuss the topic. The teacher interjects and provides commentary, highlighting positive aspects (e.g., turn-taking, active listening, building on others' comments) and offers suggestions (e.g., using peers' names, inviting others to say more). This quick activity can be done repeatedly and focus on different aspects of small group discussion to constantly improve interactions and learning.

Classroom Trials and Debate

We have written extensively over the years on the power of classroom court trials and forensic debate (Morrell, 2003). Quite simply, because we love these activity settings! They are engaging, students develop strong oral skills that allow them to shape powerful arguments, they build teamwork, and they help students to understand that there are multiple sides to an argument and very intelligent people can come to reasonable, if opposing conclusions while analyzing evidence. We include trials and debates in this chapter because they remain on the periphery of classroom life. While they may not dominate the structure of our classrooms like large and small group discussions, we believe trials and debates have an important role to play in the polyvocal classroom.

Debates can be quickly put together. Ernest would ask a question or present a topic and divide the class into two groups. The groups would have a period of time to develop their arguments, decide who would present in the short rounds, who would rebut, who would gather evidence, and who would record notes that could be used in closing arguments. All of this could happen in one extended class period. Following is an example of debate rounds in a sixty-minute classroom period:

Opening Statements

10:25—10:30—Team 1 makes an opening statement stating their position
10:30—10:35—Team 2 makes an opening statement stating their position

Round 1

10:35—10:40—Team 1 chooses one person to give one particular example
10:40—10:43—Team 2 rebuts the position

Round 2

10:43—10:48—Team 2 chooses one person to give one particular example
10:48—10:53—Team 1 rebuts the position

Round 3

10:53—10:58—Team 1 chooses one person to give one particular example
10:58—11:01—Team 2 rebuts the position

Round 4

11:01—11:06—Team 2 chooses one person to give one particular example
11:06—11:09—Team 1 rebuts the position

Closing comments

11:09—11:15—Teams regroup to prepare closing arguments
11:15—11:20—Team 2 (or 1) gives closing comments
11:20—11:25—Team 1 (or 2) gives closing comments

Of course, this is just one suggestion for a format and times can be lengthened or tightened depending on the class period, but it is possible to have great debates in a limited amount of time! Court trials take longer, but they can also be great fun. Ernest would give a few days to prepare. The trials usually lasted two weeks and followed an elaborate format that developed over time. At the culmination of the literary work, students were given the trial assignment and the class would be split into two groups. The teams would have a few days to prepare and each group would have specific tasks. They would select students to play the witnesses. They would also select their attorneys. Attorneys were only allowed to question or cross-examine one witness, providing more agentive roles. Each side also chose lawyers' assistants who would perform background research and help to prepare witnesses for cross-examination from the opposing side. With the large number of roles, everyone in a class of 30–35 students could meaningfully participate as a witness, an attorney, or an attorney's assistant.

Improving Multimodal Presentations

The ultimate manifestation of voice in the polyvocal classroom features students as public intellectuals and disseminators of knowledge. Whether giving a short research report, a book talk, reciting a poem, or acting out a student-produced play, there are many opportunities to present to peers and the larger community. To be successful, students must have ample practice speaking in whole groups, small groups and debates and they must understand the three elements of Aristotle's rhetorical triangle: ethos (speaker), pathos (audience), and logos (message). For multimodal presentations, they need to consider what they say as much as how they share their work, meaning how they use their voice, speak from the diaphragm, and employ positive body language. These skills should be explicitly taught and practiced. Ernest would introduce vocal exercises that were as simple as having students stand up and say their name and their favorite color. Students would also practice their posture and how to speak from notes and slides while not turning their back to their audience. The more students practice voice, posture, and blocking, the more confident they feel when making formal presentations and speaking to larger audiences.

As a literacy specialist, Jodene worked with a group of sixth graders who were supposed to be reading *Walk Two Moons* (Creech, 1994) with their class but had read ahead and finished on their own. Collectively, they selected to read *Stowaway* (Hesse, 2000) but after a few weeks they lost interest, voted to stop reading, and instead created projects aligned with the book. Each student submitted a plan outlining connections to the novel, materials, a timeline, and their own rubric. The final projects included a rap song, PowerPoint presentation, script and videotaped play, scrapbook with photographs and captions chronicling the novel, and an alternative final chapter. The students participated in each other's projects, created a presentation script, presented their projects to the three sixth-grade classes, family members, and faculty. For weeks they revised project plans, wrote scripts and chapters, read about the novel's time period, learned how to make a short film, and scripted lyrics. Each student also wrote a final reflection discussing their process and product. The volume and energy in our classroom were high and each student linked their passion (e.g., film making, rap, scrapbooking, writing) to their multimodal projects, improved their public speaking skills, considered their audience, engaged in meaningful dialogue with peers, and wrote extensively. They exhibited the excitement, motivation, and engagement we desire to see each day in our classrooms.

The twenty-first-century English classroom is quickly becoming a space of multimodal production and polyvocality. When we open up spaces for students to speak truth, to listen carefully, to produce new meanings, and to wonder collectively, we will have the responsive and engaging classrooms we want and need. We are on our way. Our discipline has a powerful tradition of pushing pedagogy in ways that center students and that privileges critical questioning and the power of language. Making ubiquitous the culturally responsive polyvocal classroom is our next step on this beautiful journey.

CHAPTER FIVE

Critical Family Engagement in Reading Multicultural Literature

An elementary school is hosting its first Fall Family Literacy Night (FLN). The FLN committee designed flyers, to which several students added illustrations, and the flyer was translated into Spanish and Vietnamese—the two dominant home languages of their students. They added a page to the website and emailed parents a copy of the flyer. Two weeks before the event, all the teachers included flyers in the students' home communication folders and encouraged the children to share the flyer with their family and to ask them to attend. The teachers also told students to inform their families that the Parent Teacher Association was providing drinks and snacks, childcare for younger siblings, and a drawing for books and other literacy-related materials. One week before the event, another flyer was included in students' home communication folders as a reminder. On the day of the FLN, students designed posters for their classrooms, the halls, and the front door of the school to welcome families. The event began in the auditorium where the Principal thanked families for attending, younger siblings could go with an adult to a classroom for read alouds and activities, and a librarian from the local public library talked about all the resources at the library and brought library card applications that families could complete and give to her or take home with them and then visit their local branch to get library cards. Student volunteers then served as "tour guides" and escorted families to various classrooms for twenty-minute sessions where they could learn about interactive read alouds and participate in literacy activities that they could do at home. After an hour (three activities) families reconvened in the auditorium where the drawing was held and families won books and gift cards to a local bookstore. Families, students, and teachers had the opportunity to talk and enjoy drinks and a snack before the Principal thanked everyone for attending, reminded them to fill out an application for a library card or take the application with them, and to watch for the flyer for their spring Family Literacy Night. The Principal asked families to fill out a brief survey so they could make their Spring FLN even more successful. Families left with baggies of materials for home literacy activities, new ideas for making read alouds a part of their daily lives, and another touchpoint with the school—whittling down the divide between home and school. The day after the FLN, the faculty met to discuss the event— particularly what went well and what they could change and improve upon for the Spring FLN.

If we did not understand the valuable role parents played in the literate lives of their children before the Covid crisis, we certainly do now. The worldwide pandemic essentially closed schools from March 2020 through most of the 2020–21 academic year and required far more dependency on the homes and families to transmit valuable classroom content to children. While the epidemic is a short-term reality and most children are back in classrooms in person, it behooves us to understand how best to *critically* engage parents and families for the long haul around the uses of multicultural children's and young adult literature in the home.

This chapter considers what *critical family engagement* around multicultural literature might look like. A critical approach begins by reenvisioning parents and caregivers as informed and empowered partners in the literacy learning of their children (Mapp, 2011; Souto-Manning, 2004). A critical approach should further enable family members to create meaningful and dialogic relationships with teachers and schools that are situated more in reciprocity, mutual respect, and love than in a banking method of parent-to-teacher transmission (Freire, 1998). We further argue, along with Friere's message to teachers in *Teachers as Cultural Workers* (1997) that the best teachers are continuous learners and, for the best interest of the students, a huge part of that continual learning involves resituating parents as experts and partners. Toward these ends, we are guided by Karen Mapp's *Dual Capacity Framework* (Mapp & Kuttner, 2013) where schools and staff: (1) honor and recognize families' funds of knowledge; (2) connect family engagement to student learning; and (3) create welcoming, inviting cultures. Mapp also advocates that families negotiate multiple roles including: *Supporters, Encouragers, Monitors, Advocates, Decision Makers,* and *Collaborators.*

A critical approach to family engagement centers school-home dialogue, choice, community cultural wealth, storytelling, and critical joy. Students and their caregivers should only be involved in collective activities that are responsive to their needs and interests. Students should spend most of their time at home reading what interests them and family members should spend their time bathing their children in love and support. A critical family engagement advocates for meaningful dialogue pertaining to the act of reading and the themes and issues that arise in the texts that circulate in read alouds and choice reading. Parents and other caregivers are ideally situated to be supportive and critical interlocutors with the diverse literature children consume and they can encourage thoughtful reflection and action based upon their readings of texts in the home.

Finally, a critical approach to family literacy engagement facilitates a liberatory consciousness where families and students collaboratively renegotiate their relationship to the word and the world via their co-readings of children's literary texts (Freire & Macedo, 1987). Classroom teachers have an important role to play in fostering an increased engagement with multicultural literature in the home. We will discuss relevant research, how teachers can encourage more reading aloud, choice, and independent reading in the home. We will further explore the role of interactive culturally responsive read alouds and multicultural literature, and how teachers can help address the barriers to joyful reading experiences between adult family members and students at home. We conclude by discussing the Family-Super-Reader pledge and ideas for enhancing Family Literacy Nights.

The Power of Outside of School Reading

If adult family members encourage their children to read independently for ten minutes a day during the school year and thirty minutes a day during the summer, the growth in reading achievement is tremendous [Beers & Probst, 2017, citing Anderson, Wilson & Fielding (1988)]. Studies dating back to the mid-1980s corroborate these magic numbers. For example, Anderson, Wilson, and Fielding (1988) found "staggering" differences in the amount of time kids read outside of school. Based on data from 155 fifth-grade students from seven classrooms, their most startling findings was, "the child who is at the 90th percentile in amount of book reading spends nearly five times as many minutes per day reading books as the child at the 50th percentile, and over two hundred times as many minutes per day reading books as the child at the 10th percentile" (p. 296). Considering all a child learns and gains during those minutes, such as increased vocabulary, comprehension, and reading speed, ten minutes a day during the school year and thirty minutes a day during the summer are miniscule blocks of time for tremendous literacy gains.

Outside of school, students should choose books they enjoy and can read fluently. Steven Krashen's meta-study of reading research identifies the amount of reading students do on their own and by choice as the most important variables in determining reading achievement. The field refers to this as "independent reading," but we prefer to identify these moments as "choice reading." We imagine children and adolescents reading freely and fluently and enjoying what they read and the very act of being competent and empowered readers. This simply will not happen for children and adolescents unless independent or choice reading in the home becomes ubiquitous. Perhaps the lowest hanging fruit in the scramble to increase reading joy and reading outcomes is to increase the amount of independent choice reading that happens in the classroom and home.

The companion to choice reading is the read aloud. In a 2018 Literacy Leadership Brief, the International Literacy Association identified the two most solid research-based practices in literacy education to be independent reading and the read aloud. Read alouds have been variously defined over the past forty years. We prefer the definition from the classic *Becoming a Nation of Readers* (Anderson, Hiebert, Scott & Wilkinson, 1985) that defines the read aloud as: A strategy in which a teacher or parent sets aside time to read orally to students on a consistent basis texts above their independent reading level, but at their listening level. This definition identifies four key components of a read aloud.

First, the read aloud involves a teacher, parent, older sibling or adult who acts as a reading role model. Lester Laminack (2009) argues that, even more than the book, the relationship with a caring adult compels children and adolescents to be drawn to the read aloud. During that moment, the world stops and they have the undivided attention of someone they love or respect. We will say more on the importance of the reading sponsor later. Second, the oral nature of the read aloud enables students to listen to a story. Oral storytelling is as old as the human tradition. Nothing is more natural to our sense of ourselves in the world than hearing stories. Henry Louis Gates (2012) argues we are etched into being through story. While book reading may seem new and even contrived to students, hearing elders tell a story is a reassuring experience and allows the transmission of culture and academic vocabulary. Third, read alouds are most effective when they happen consistently. For some families, this may be bedtime or a set aside moment in the mornings or evenings. Regardless of the time of day, ideally they happen as often as possible as a normal element of home and community life. Reading aloud at home should continue, even when children can read independently; yet one in four parents of children between ages six and seventeen stop reading aloud to their children before the age of nine (Scholastic, 2019). Finally, when possible, read alouds should come from texts that are above the children's independent reading level, but at their listening level. Read alouds allow children and adolescents access to texts that might be beyond them without the help of their reading sponsor. Whether it is a parent, grandparent, or other adult caregiver reading a letter from a distant relative, a reading from a sacred or religious text, or working through classic series like *Lord of the Rings* (Tolkier, 1968), *Harry Potter and the Philosopher's Stone* (Rowling, 1997), or *Chronicles of Narnia* (Lewis, 1950), or using Mildred Taylor's *Role of Thunder, Hear My Cry* (1976) to explain to younger children what it was like to grow up in America during Jim Crow segregation, read alouds open up a whole new world to the children that are lucky enough to experience them regularly.

The research is unequivocal on the myriad benefits of the read aloud. For this chapter, we focus on just four: (1) reading aloud builds reader identities; (2) reading aloud, more than talking, builds literacy; (3) reading aloud builds background knowledge; and (4) reading aloud builds vocabulary.

Reading Aloud Builds
Reader Identities

Pioneering literacy researcher P. David Pearson points to reader identity as the biggest predictor of reading success. A child who identifies as a reader reads more often for pleasure and takes risks that one needs to become a proficient reader. Read alouds build knowledge for future reading success (*Becoming a Nation of Readers*, 1985) by teaching children of all ages to associate reading with pleasure and providing a reading role model, while developing vocabulary and background knowledge. It also builds classroom community around shared experiences; develops speaking, listening, and attention skills; and widens students' views of the world.

Reading Aloud, More than Talking, Builds Literacy

Dominic Massaro, a professor emeritus who studies language acquisition and literacy, found that although parents can build their children's vocabularies by talking to them, reading to them is more effective. Reading aloud is the best way to help children develop word mastery and grammatical understanding, which form the basis for learning how to read. Massaro (2016) found picture books are two to three times as likely as parent-child conversations to include a word that isn't among the 5,000 most common English words. Additionally, picture books include even more uncommon words than conversations among adults. In the study, Massaro compared the words in 112 popular picture books to adult-to-child conversations and adult-to-adult conversations. The picture books included such favorites as *Goodnight Moon* (Brown, 1947) and *If You Give a Mouse a Cookie* (Numeroff, 1985).

Building literacy through read alouds is highly effective and supportive for children learning English as a new language, especially picture books with illustrations or photographs aligning closely with the printed text to provide context clues. Children typically have opportunities to hear and practice conversational English during the school day (before and after school; recess), which develops quicker than academic language, making the read aloud in English an important literacy activity during school. Students can hear and see a teacher model reading in English in a low stakes activity without worrying about answering questions or writing a response. While listening, they are learning academic registers not frequently heard in everyday conversations (Giroir, Grimaldo, Vaughn & Roberts, 2015). Teachers can also integrate highly effective strategies for teaching English with read alouds including "teaching vocabulary in context, facilitating negotiated interaction around text, and sustaining linguistically and culturally relevant learning environments" (Giroir et al., 2015, p. 640).

At home, read alouds should be conducted as often as possible in the family's home language. Many of the skills we teach in school such as making predictions, identifying author's craft, summarizing, evaluating, and making text connections, can be done in any language. This also honors the home language and does not compromise child-parent relationships by having a child understand more English than the adult. Ideally this helps children maintain their home language and nurtures child-adult caregiver relationships while developing literacy skills that can transfer to reading and writing in English.

Read Alouds Build Background Knowledge

The read aloud and follow-up conversations allow teachers opportunities to help students develop background knowledge and connect concepts so they can clarify their thinking during their discussions with their peers and teacher (Dorn & Soffos, 2005). Renowned literacy scholar Richard Allington (2001) agrees and writes that for children to develop thoughtful literacy, they must be given an abundant number of opportunities throughout the day to demonstrate their understanding and practice using comprehension strategies under the teacher's guidance. Read alouds also stimulate curiosity in children as they are invited into a safe environment to marvel at the concepts being presented (Harvey, 1998).

Read Alouds Build Vocabulary

Many studies have identified a class-based academic vocabulary in elementary classrooms (Chall, Jacobs & Baldwin, 1990; Snow, Burns & Griffin, 1998). Routman (2003) found that reading aloud to children enables them to hear the rich language of stories and texts they cannot yet read on their own. By reading aloud to students, they learn new vocabulary, grammar, and information and how stories and written language works. Some of the other research benefits of reading aloud includes improved classroom climate, an increased desire in students to read on their own, improved reading comprehension, an increase in curiosity and critical thinking, and better academic outcomes. While read alouds are often associated with younger readers, research reveals that classrooms with interactive read alouds yield similar effects for upper grades and across disciplines.

Anderson et al.'s (1988) most "newsworthy" finding from their study was the teacher's significant influence on the amount of book reading children do out of school. When they recorded the average amount of time teachers spent reading aloud to their class, the most was 16.5 minutes per day and the least was 4.1 minutes per day (p. 296). They found strong correlations between the amount of time a teacher read aloud to their students and the child's reading comprehension and vocabulary. They also shared ways that teachers in their study promoted reading including "access to interesting books at a suitable level of difficulty, using incentives to increase motivation for reading, reading aloud to children, and providing time for reading during the school day" (p. 297). Little has changed in how teachers encourage students to read more in and out of school over the past thirty years.

The Culturally Responsive Read Aloud

Rudine Sims Bishop (1990), renowned scholar of multicultural children's literature, is often cited for her analogy of multicultural literature to windows, mirrors, and sliding glass doors. She describes books as windows which offer "views of worlds that may be real or imagined, familiar or strange." These windows can become sliding glass doors which readers can walk through and become completely immersed in a different world. A window can also serve as a mirror, "when lighting conditions are just right" and in the literature, "we can see our own lives and experiences as part of the larger human experience" (p. 1). When teachers and adult family members help select a wide range of multicultural texts as read alouds, they create spaces for rich conversations about the child's experiences and perspectives and can serve as windows, mirrors, and sliding glass doors. Ebony Thomas (2016) cautions that "when children grow up without seeing diverse images in the mirrors, windows, and doors of children's literature (Bishop, 1990), it limits them to single stories about the world around them (Adichie, 2009) and ultimately affects the development of their imaginations" (p. 112).

Culturally responsive read alouds may be interpreted as literature that only reflects a child's lived experiences such as having characters that perfectly match the child's cultural, linguistic, ethnic, and social background but that is not what we are suggesting. While we want children to see themselves in the books they read themselves or enjoy as read alouds, a variety of texts can help children recognize similarities of positive and similar experiences with children of various backgrounds (Copenhaver-Johnson, 2006). As they are making text connections (text-self, text-text, text-world), they are looking for similarities and differences to find common ground and appreciate diversity. Whether the characters, plot, or setting are familiar or different from the child's world, the read aloud provides a space for the child to share their own stories in comparison to the book (Allyn & Morrell, 2016). This also allows for children to bring their outside experiences and lives into the classroom and school life (Copenhaver-Johnson, 2006) as they seek connections with the literature.

The number of books receiving notable and prestigious awards such as the Caldecott Medal, Newbery Medal, Coretta Scott King Book Award, or Pura Belpré Award, to name a few, feature far more characters of color and are being written and illustrated by more authors and illustrators of color (Cooperative Children's Book Center, 2020). In fact, in 2018, the Newbery winner and honor books were all written by authors of color and featured many ethnically and culturally diverse characters and cultures. When we consider the shifting demographics of our K-12 population, which is now approximately 54 percent non-white and projected to increase to 56 percent by 2029 (NCES, 2022), we can appreciate the need for diverse books and opportunities for children to see themselves in books. When these types of books, which celebrate people and communities of color in authentic ways, are shared as read alouds, the child is more likely to develop a positive racial identity. Wanless and Crawford (2016) assert that this type of book, "Allows readers to see different aspects of themselves, their communities, and the people they love." These stories, particularly ones that address social justice issues and feature ethnically, culturally, linguistically, and socioeconomically diverse characters and communities, can help children move from color-blindness to color-awareness to deeper understandings about social justice (Laminack & Wadsworth, 2012; Paley, 2000). With the read aloud, family members or teachers can model for the child(ren) about how to talk about injustice (Copenhaver-Johnson, 2006). Culturally responsive read alouds expose children to people, communities, and stories that may be very similar or different from their own which opens space for dialogue to find connections, identify differences, and celebrate what makes them and their experiences valuable.

The Super Reader Pledge

Clearly multicultural literature can be a centerpiece of a home life that is awash with read alouds, storytelling, and room for independent, choice reading. As educators, one of the challenges becomes understanding what barriers might exist to enacting these practices in home and community settings and working with families to remove those barriers.

There are too many other cumbersome things we ask parents and other caregivers to do that makes their reading relationships with their children more stressful than they need to be. We should stop asking family members to be teachers, homework helpers, and disciplinarians around academic performance and, instead, allow them to have joyful experiences around reading in the home.

We know that the population of students is becoming poorer as the years go by. Currently, half of our students live within 200 percent of the federal poverty line, which equates to an income of $26,000 for a family of four. Poorer children also have adult family members and caregivers who are often recipients of an impoverished education and who also hold negative perceptions of themselves as readers and writers and students in general. We must face the reality that parents often know they should read to their children, but they feel incompetent and insecure about their ability to do so.

Acknowledging this reality can help us tremendously as we remove clutter from the family-child-school relationship and as we work to build confidence and capacity in parents so that they can have meaningful and joy-filled reading relationships with their children. In *Every Child a Super Reader*, Pam Allyn and Ernest Morrell (2016) offered a strengths-based approach to develop the joy of reading in our most vulnerable children. Part of that work offered ways for teachers to work with parents to reinforce these same strengths in the home. One result of that work is a parent Super Reader pledge that embraces the research around reading achievement, the research on powerful social emotional learning and combines those discourses with a model of parent-engagement that promotes positivity, confidence, and capacity. The ten components of the Super Reader pledge are:

1 Ten minutes of independent reading each night
2 Ten minutes of child-centered discussion each night
3 Thirty minutes of reading each day during the summer (1000 hours)
4 Creating a personalized book basket for my child
5 Getting and using a local library card
6 Being a reading role model for my child
7 Promote socio emotional skills and community
8 Creating a home environment where reading is cherished
9 Participate in a school or local library summer reading program
10 Participate in my child's Family Literacy Nights at school

None of these components requires families to be anything other than advocates and cheerleaders for their children's literacy learning. We acknowledge many parents are justifiably concerned about their own reading ability. We also acknowledge some family members are not speakers of English as a first or second language. Toward those ends, we focus on how families can create a home environment that is filled with texts and with conversations about texts and a home that celebrates reading as a necessary part of the everyday life of the home. Each component also allows teachers to communicate with parents about literacy research that supports these recommendations. We present to families the Anderson study and Krashen's work on the importance of choice and independent reading. We discuss social and emotional learning and the social emotional barriers to academic achievement (i.e., low confidence, lack of reading identity, lack of motivation, and self-isolation from a classroom or home reading community), and we share best practices for improving a joy of reading, an empowered reading identity, and set of family norms that allow children to develop a reading stamina, an academic vocabulary, and reading fluency.

The Family Literacy Nights

A related component of the work with families are Family Literacy Nights. These nights are great ways for teachers to share books and resources that might be useful for parents; they are an ideal way to learn from parents about their triumphs, their fears and concerns as they relate to engaging their children around reading; and, most importantly, they are a wonderful way to build relationships between parents and teachers as partners in the literacy learning of children. We suggest having food, childcare, and giveaways for family members, if possible. Ernest would often joke that Chick-Fil-A and childcare will get families out. One evening he and Pam Allyn were presenting to a rural county school district near Blacksburg, Virginia, home of Virginia Tech University. This is significant because Virginia Tech was playing in the first round of the NCAA Tournament the night of the scheduled event. The school did provide Chick-Fil-A for the whole family, child care was provided by older children, and activities for younger children while their parents met in the gymnasium. Well the gym was standing room only. Families occupied every seat and lined up wall to wall as Pam and Ernest shared the

Super Reader work and offered the pledge for parents to take. They shared research, simple strategies we hoped would be low stress and full of joy, and we answered their questions about building confidence in their children who were already developing low confidence as readers. They shared ideas for great books for kids and online resources where they could ask for recommendations for books as well as online sites that had excellent read alouds.

Ernest visited a district in Northern Texas to share with teachers ideas for engaging parents and he mentioned the Family Literacy Nights and the Super Reader pledge. The teachers had Superman-like T-shirts that they wore to the professional learning days and they developed the superhero theme to last throughout the year. During their first Family Literacy Night they wrote out the Super Reader family pledge on large construction paper and had all of the parents sign the pledge, which they then used to line the entire corridor that led to the administrative offices. Every day as children traversed that hallway they could see their adult family members' signatures on that Super Reader pledge. Whenever family members visited the school they relived the collective agreement they made. How cool is that?

Best Practices for Family Literacy Nights (Three or Four Times a Year)

1 Food
2 Childcare and activities for children
3 Free books and other giveaways for family members
4 Discussion of adult caregivers' reading identities
5 Sharing data on value of reading at home
6 Discussion of interactive and responsive read alouds
7 Discussion of independent reading time and student choice

8   Sharing resources for getting great recommendations for children's and young adult literature

9   Discussion of strategies for using the school and community libraries and adding to home libraries

10 Taking the pledge

The separation between school and home has varied a great deal over time and across communities, but has likely never been as blurred as in recent times with the pandemic. Schools have leaned on families to do far more at home, much of what was previously relegated to the classroom and teachers. While schools have often asked families to reinforce what is taught at school, such as completing homework and reading aloud with their child and filling in reading logs, families have been asked to do far more—everything from learning new technology, sitting with their children to support their learning, checking over work and submitting work, while still being expected to have their child read on their own and on a consistent basis. Some family members have not felt prepared to take on more of a teacher's role during distance learning and under "normal" circumstances, would not be expected to do so. However, one positive and perhaps unintended consequence of distance learning has been more attention to thinking about how to support families as they support their children's learning at home.

We have intended to highlight and share ways for families to situate joy at the center of their reading activities with their children. Rather than asking families to be teachers, we suggest teachers and school leaders encourage more natural ways to build a love of reading through storytelling, reading together, and encouraging children to independently read books that motivate and excite them. Our suggestions are supported by decades of research in literacy teaching and learning, social emotional learning, and engagement and motivation. Our suggestions are also inexpensive, such as getting a free library card and visiting the local library on a regular basis, and do not require significant time.

CHAPTER SIX

Conclusion: The Future of Children's Literature Is Already Here

Three middle-school students are huddled together, pointing at a graphic novel in the center of the desk, talking over one another, heads practically touching. The student who borrowed the manga One Piece (Volume 1; Chapter 1–7) by Eiichiro Oda, from his local library, is explaining how the East Blue Saga includes six arcs and how each arc is represented by the chapters and volumes in the manga. Another student asks how his friend knows all these details, besides watching the anime and fans' videos on his phone every day. One student comments on how it takes "forever" to get through the episodes because of the fillers and another student agrees but then admits that he likes knowing the characters' backstories because it helps him to understand their motives. Since they are at different points in watching the 1,011 (as of April 2022) episodes of the most popular and remunerative anime of all time, they agree "no spoilers" and only discuss up to the episode that everyone has seen. The bell rings and they continue looking at the manga, debating when Luffy will become the "King of the Pirates," who are the best characters and fight scenes— not noticing their teacher who is walking over to the desk. As it turns out, the teacher is ahead of the students in watching the anime and has been brainstorming ways to encourage his students to seriously consider becoming graphic artists—to produce both anime (animation) and manga (graphic novels). He is determined to turn the class into a "maker space" and reimagine what it means to be "literate," what is considered "literacy" and how to engage, excite, and motivate his students to invest their talents and passion into their work for a wide audience. He announces to the class that they will be visited by two local graphic artists and for their next unit, which will focus on Kwame Alexander's The Crossover (both poetic form and graphic novel) to explore themes including "coming of age," the roles of family members, and child agency, they will be creating their own graphic novels which will be shared and on display in their school library and local public library. The room erupts into excited chatter, especially from the students who were discussing One Piece.

We began the book discussing a fourth-grade classroom where students were developing their own multimedia projects based on themes from Christopher Paul Curtis's novel *Bud, Not Buddy*. The teacher was deeply committed to building a beloved community where Belonging, along with the six other *Super Reader* strengths (Friendship, Kindness, Curiosity, Confidence, Courage, and Hope) (Allyn & Morrell, 2022) shaped not just her pedagogy, but every interaction between students and between the students and teacher. Her Freirian approach, which encouraged students to be heard and actionable, manifested in how they engaged in deep critical readings of multicultural literature together and choices for how they could show their understanding and connections to the novel (e.g., creating video games, writing their own hip-hop albums, developing podcasts). Having a wide audience, beyond the classroom walls, and developing skills and knowledge around media consumption, production, and dissemination was this teacher's approach to ensuring her students knew they were important and loved within the classroom. It began with a sincere desire to learn more about how her students spent their time outside of school that she could then bring into the classroom to capitalize on their interests and expertise which would in turn deepen their knowledge of literacy and literature (Emdin, 2016; Ladson-Billings, 1994). To be clear, while she was learning from her students and deepening her own knowledge about her students' lives outside of school as well as their interests such as digital media production and popular culture, she still maintained authority and responsibility for their learning. In a published conversation with long-time friend Donaldo Macedo in 1995, a conversation that began in 1983, Paulo Freire stated, "Teachers maintain a certain level of authority through the depth and breadth of knowledge of the subject matter that they teach" (p. 378), addressing the misconception of what it means to democratize power in the classroom. While teachers should be learning more about their students, as a means to teach, Freire clearly states, "There is no educational practice that does not point to an objective; this proves that the nature of educational practice has direction" (p. 378). Learning from students and encouraging them to play a collaborative role in a project-based approach to literacy engagement and learning is not the same as laissez-faire pedagogy. Teachers must maintain a certain level of pedagogical authority and responsibility and not become merely a facilitator, thereby relinquishing any form of authority or knowledge. According to Freire, that would be disingenuous. Alternatively, Freire cautions that "educators should never allow their active and curious presence to transform the learners' presence into a shadow of the educator's presence" (p. 379). Therefore, if we wish to enact a Freirian approach, we need to ask how young people are spending their time outside of school and draw on their passions to maximize their engagement, motivation, agency, voice, and joy with a clear direction and objectives in mind and always acting in the role of teacher, not facilitator.

Assuming the fourth graders in our Introduction opening vignette are like most eight–twelve-year-olds, they would be spending approximately fifty-five minutes each day playing computer and console games and thirty minutes playing mobile games (Boston Children's Hospital—Digital Wellness Lab, 2022). We are well aware of how critical media theorists have documented the negative effects from too much access to the corporate media (Giroux, 2010; Steinberg, 2011). However, there are also benefits to youth critically engaging digital media (i.e., playing video games) that we often hear about less, such as the development of digital literacies (Gee, 2003) improved motor functioning, motor skills, prosocial behavior (e.g., sharing and learning by pitching in) (Rivero & Gutierrez, 2022) and social interactions (connection and community) which can reduce loneliness and anxiety. The year 2022 marks fifty years since the first video arcade game, Pong, was commercially released. Since 1972, gaming has expanded to include a myriad of platforms (Cloud, VR, Handheld, Mobile, PC, Arcade, and Console) to become a $165 billion industry—outpacing film and television (Visual Capitalist, 2020). Rather than lamenting the amount of time our students are spending on gaming, how can we tap into the benefits of this world of entertainment and learning? And, rather than claiming that literacy and reading are moving targets, a more accurate critique of these terms and what they encompass is to acknowledge that they are constantly evolving and responding to cultural, technological, and changing purposes. Video game developers, publishers, authors, artists, and booksellers are acutely aware of these influences and respond by producing texts (digital and traditional) that appeal and respond to the interests and demands of consumers.

If you visit your local brick and mortar bookstore, particularly large chain stores, you are likely to find that the "Fantasy," "Anime," "Manga," and "Gaming" sections have grown significantly. The anime section is likely to include *One Piece* manga (comics or graphic novel) books, the most popular manga of all time with over 500 million volumes in circulation worldwide (Statistics & Data, 2022). In fact, when doing a Google search for Barnes and Noble (online search, 6/20/2022), the first category below the name, link to their website, and brief description of the bookseller is "Manga and Anime Books." It is also worth noting that Amazon continues to lead the world in book sales and continues to innovate with social platforms such as Goodreads and the Kindle Cloud Reader to expand their sale of traditional books (hardcover and paperback) to include e-books. Outside of schools, publishers and booksellers have innovated and included digital options to entice readers. How can we do the same in the classroom?

Often when we think about literature for children, "classics" such as *Charlotte's Web* (E. B. White), *Charlie and the Chocolate Factory* (Roald Dahl), or *Goodnight Moon* (Margaret Wise Brown) come to mind, or those donning gold and silver stickers of the most recognized awards including the John Newbery, Randolph Caldecott, Pura Belpré, or Coretta Scott King Award. "Classic" implies traditional print books. What we want to be asking is "What are kids reading by choice?" While adults might cringe at the thought of a child spending hours reading *Diary of a Wimpy Kid* (Jeff Kinney), as of 2021, the series had sold over 250 million copies worldwide and ranked as the sixth best-selling book series of all time. The series won the Nickelodeon Kids' Choice Award every year from 2008 to 2016, which is awarded based on votes from viewers worldwide. Likewise, the first book in the Harry Potter series, *Harry Potter and the Philosopher's Stone* (Rowling, 1997) has sold approximately 120 million copies—after *Tale of Two Cities* (Dickens, 1859) and *The Little Prince* (Saint-Exupery, 1943). Neither Kinney's nor Rowlings' books would be considered classic literature and while they might be found in classroom and school libraries, rarely would they be taught as part of an English Language Arts program. We are not arguing that they should, but we would suggest that *what* we are teaching and *how* we are teaching does not always align with what brings joy, excitement, and engagement for many students. We only need to look as far as Barnes and Nobles and leading publishers such as *Scholastic* to understand what young readers are devouring, which is primarily graphic novels, gaming, fantasy, and anime-manga. So what are kids reading and what sells?

Manga, an umbrella term for a variety of comic books and graphic novels originally produced and published in Japan (Pagan, 2018) experienced a sales increase of 40 percent in 2020 in the United States. Globally, the comic book industry is worth approximately $7.14 billion. Fifty-four percent of the global comic book market comes from Japan and South Korea. While not quite at the magnitude of the Asian manga industry (approximately $5.6 billion) the United States has seen consistent growth and reached a revenue of $1.21 billion in 2019. MarketWatch predicts that based on recent growth, the comic book industry will continue to grow at 3.3 percent annually and by 2026, reach $4,686.2 million (Kentic, 2021).

The United States readership of manga is heavily concentrated among a younger generation (Kentic, 2021). While manga is an umbrella term for comic books and graphic novels, style, stories, and characters are tailored for various audiences and like most literature for children, content is based on imagined readers' age and gender (Reynolds, 2011). According to TV Tropes, "Children aged ten or younger generally read Kodomo manga, while teenagers turn to somewhat more serious Shonen or Shoujo manga. Shonen is intended for boys, while Shoujo manga is aimed at female teenagers" (TV Tropes, 2022). In 2021, the most popular and best-selling Shonen manga series of all time, *One Piece* (Eiichiro Oda) sold over 490 million copies worldwide, with 400 million in Japan and 90 million copies in 57 countries and regions overseas (Loo, 2021).

We are not suggesting that educators eliminate enduring children's literary classics. However, we encourage educators to pause and consider why, over the past thirty years, the same novels continue to make the top ten lists. A large-scale survey by the National Center on Literature Teaching and Learning in 1988, which was then written and published as a report by Arthur Applebee in 1989, included 488 public, Catholic, and independent schools and found that the four most commonly taught novels were *Romeo and Juliet, Huckleberry*

Finn, MacBeth, and *Scarlet Letter.* Over two decades later, Stallworth (2012) found that the most frequently taught book-length works by six- to twelve-grade ELA and English teachers in nine southeastern states were *The Great Gatsby, Romeo and Juliet, The Crucible, The Odyssey, To Kill a Mockingbird,* and *Night.* In her article, she mentions the most frequently read books in a study from 2006 included *The Scarlet Letter, The Great Gatsby, To Kill a Mockingbird,* and *The Scarlet Letter.* Given the expansive range of novels available to middle and secondary ELA and English teachers, the canon has remained remarkably narrow over the past several decades. While each novel mentioned in the surveys has its merits and deserves consideration as part of a literary canon for six- to twelve-grade ELA and English classes, broadening the genre and format to include more recently published texts may speak more powerfully to today's students. For example, we believe Shakespeare should be included on the syllabus; however, why not consider graphic novel series (fourteen plays currently available) such as *Manga Shakespeare,* which include the words verbatim but in a format that engages today's students. Not only do these types of texts represent a multicultural perspective and images, they speak to students in a format they are more likely to choose on their own.

Rather than becoming discouraged by headlines such as "Among many U.S. children, reading for fun has become less common, federal data shows" (Schaeffer, 2021) we should be asking what children are reading outside of school, how they are spending their free time, the role of literacy in their everyday lives, and how we bring these into the classroom. How can we tap into and capitalize on the joy and engagement they experience in literacy rich experiences outside of school? What can we learn from publishers' top selling book lists and the layout and books on the shelves at local bookstores? These corporate entities are economically invested in knowing the answers to these questions. In other words, they have done the research and it's available. As previously mentioned, we are not advocating for eliminating classics and replacing one narrow body of literature with another. Instead, we are suggesting we draw on the findings of national surveys by the Pew Research Center, the National Assessment of Educational Progress and others. This begs the question of what might these look like in today's ELA classrooms?

When we are fully engaged in an activity we experience what Csikszentmihalyi (1990) called "flow," explained by Wilhelm and Wilhelm (2010) as "being so immersed in an activity that nothing else seems to matter"—it is "the hallmark of engagement, motivated performance, and the experience of happiness" (p. 39). Using gaming as an example, even when the activity is challenging and includes many moments of failure, kids remain engaged for hours—motivated to improve, to increase their score, gain points, defeat their nemesis, and move on to the next level. We know kids voluntarily engage in these types of activities even when they experience "failure" more times than success, such as mastering a trick on their skateboards, making a goal in soccer, or mastering a difficult piece on a musical instrument. What can we learn from the students about what motivates them to remain engaged?

As educators, we can draw on the work of Freire and consider situating our pedagogy in what Freire termed the existential experiences of the people (Freire & Macedo, 1987). Critical educators of children's literature can ask the question, how are children experiencing the world? We often start with the misconception of children's problems as what they do not know, what they do, what they cannot do and/or what they will not do. We create a context of banking education, which is based on the assumption that we, as educators, have to give students what they do not have. Instead, we should be asking how we can help them to do the things that they want to do better. How do we start with what matters to them? We can begin with the question of how children are experiencing the world as literate beings and we are likely to find ourselves in the world of variously digital mobile gaming, anime, manga, popular culture, and social media. These are the texts that are the interlocutors between our children and the world. Kids are grinding out volumes of anime, in some cases, series that began and ended before they were born such as Yu-gi-oh, Pokemon, Naruto, and One Piece. One way the kids experience them is through the actual graphic novels or what we used to call comics. Another way is through the series. Kids are watching them through standard Hulu, Sling, Netflix, or on their mobile phones. They're incredibly excited about these stories because they are like the characters who are also young people. When we imagine a classroom library we may envision a certain kind of picture book or chapter book and assume that is what we should see in libraries. Some classroom libraries may even have magazines like National Geographic, but what about graphic novels? What about comic books? What about the classic Marvel or DC Comics?

If we have included time in the day for students to engage in independent reading and choose their own texts, the answer is simple. We need to add manga and graphic novels to our classroom and school libraries. If we know this is what kids are reading outside of school when they have the opportunity to choose, then we simply need to bring these into our schools and classrooms. By providing time for students to choose these texts during independent reading time, we convey the message that reading should be enjoyable and elicit joy and that reading widely is an important aspect of what readers do. Likewise, students should have time to discuss their chosen independent reading with classmates—to make recommendations, to share their reflections, and to engage in thoughtful discussions about why they chose a particular text and how it spoke to them. This offers an opportunity for all children to be part of a reading community and to see themselves as engaged and active readers with valuable insights and perspectives to share with others.

Educators have a unique opportunity to transform classrooms into maker spaces. We can begin by asking what we want our students to learn and do. How do we simultaneously guide students in becoming critical gamers while capitalizing on the elements of gaming that build and improve students' critical thinking and literacy skills. Despite doom and gloom stories on how kids are not reading as much, we can reimagine new ways that kids are consuming and producing texts through social media. For example, there are entire websites and pages for anime and manga series such as *One Piece*. Fans can learn general information about the overall organization of the anime—specifically the chapters and volumes by sagas and arcs on sites such as *One Piece Wiki*. Fans can also visit sites such as Reddit to view video clips and read through thought provoking comments. For example, one site member on Reddit submitted a comment titled "TikTok Creators have been trying to ruin the reputation of One Piece by labeling it racist" and received 1.7K comments. The commenter said:

> As a Black male I heavily disagree, the reason they are saying this is because the features on some black characters are overly exaggerated. I disagree with this being racism because Oda doesn't just put these exaggerated features on black characters. He's done the same features on characters like number 3, Don Krieg, and the Giants. Not to mention discrimination is literally one of the main issues tackled in the show of one piece with damn near perfect execution. I can tell some of these creators have never watched One Piece in their life. And only uses its name to get views without viewing the series. One of the major problems I have with people who do stuff like this is they make non racism related this (*sic*) racist.

These sites are loaded with texts and require a great deal of close and critical reading to understand the extensive conversations, nuances of language, and perspectives. We can ask ourselves if we are having these types of discussions in our classrooms. And are kids prepared to read social media critically? How might they respond to this comment and engage in the community discussion? Can they make a persuasive argument in support or opposition to this commenter's critique? Rather than lamenting the hours kids are spending on gaming and related social media sites outside of school, we might ask what we can learn from their activities. What makes it so exciting and engaging? How can we draw on what kids are doing outside of school to teach them to be critical consumers and producers both inside and outside of school?

Mirra, Morrell, and Filipiak (2018) offer an "updated and extended critical theory of multiliteracies that advocates moving beyond simply teaching students how to consume various media and extends into teaching students how to produce, distribute, and even invent new media forms themselves" (p. 13). Mirra, Morrell, and Filipiak make the case that teachers and students need to analyze "not only the text itself, but also the roles of the creator, the audience, and the stakeholders with interest in this power relationship" (p. 14). Imagine students critically analyzing the Reddit comment above and engaging in a discussion about the creator, who self identifies as a Black man and avid consumer of *One Piece*, the audience (other fans of *One Piece* and members of the *One Piece subreddit*), and the stakeholders (TikTok Creators) as well as issues of racism. His critique is provocative and generated over 1,700 responses from site members who may have initially read his comment out of curiosity—a natural human response. Freire argues that humans are by nature curious—"ontologically curious" (Freire & Macedo, 1995, p. 382). And he asserts, "Teachers who engage in an educational practice without curiosity, allowing their students to avoid engagement with critical readings, are not involved in dialogue as a process of learning and knowing" (p. 382). Teachers *and* students are endowed with curiosity which can serve as an impetus to engage in critical readings of traditional texts, digital texts, and all they read in the world. We should be encouraging students to be *more* curious (Allyn & Morrell, 2022). So rather than banning access to social media sites, which is a common practice within many districts and similar to the age-old practice of banning books, we need to prepare students to actively engage in any platform and with any text through a critical lens. We cannot micromanage all the books children read or content on social media. The most empowering approach is to teach children and young people to critically read all texts and understand how texts are promoting or challenging hegemonic dominant narratives. Then they can make informed decisions about the text and how they want to engage.

Rather than viewing students in a limited way, only as consumers of text, Mirra, Morrell, and Filipiak offer a "four-part theory of media education that includes critical digital consumption, digital production, digital distribution, and, ultimately, a pedagogy of digital invention." According to the Centers for Disease Control and Prevention (2018), kids are spending an unprecedented number of hours on screens consuming digital entertainment media. The average for children ages 8–10 is 6 hours per day, ages 11–14 is 9 hours per day, and ages 15–18 is 7.5 hours per day. The reasons and content vary; however, how they view the content and how we can create opportunities for digital production, distribution, and digital invention within the classroom applies across age groups.

Freire encouraged educators to use culture circles, spaces where students could develop their voices and share their opinions in an environment of respect and admiration (Souto-Manning, 2010). Specifically, Freire felt that culture circles should be spaces where students used their own way of speaking to verbalize their understanding of the world and subsequently how to act to change it (Souto-Manning, 2004). Mariana Souto-Manning employed Freirian culture circles in elementary classrooms to encourage students to share stories about their names, their families, their interests and desires in attempts to build community among students, between students and the teacher, and between parents and the teachers. Most importantly, the teachers in Souto-Manning's work drew upon what they learned in these circles to transform their pedagogy. We encourage literacy educators today to use Freirian culture circles to understand how and what students are reading outside of school—how they are reading the word and the world—to create learning and maker spaces within classrooms that engage students and foster supportive and encouraging environments for voice and choice. Including high interest texts in our classroom libraries such as graphic novels and manga and tapping into the elements of gaming and anime that motivate students to consume, produce, and invent text is how we should be thinking about the present and future of children's literature and literacy.

Freire, Children's Literature and Revolutionary Love

Our approach to children's literature and the work of Paulo Freire and others is guided by our commitment to revolutionary love or what Freire called "an armed loved—the fighting love of those convinced of the right and the duty to fight, to denounce, and to announce" (Freire, 1998, p. 42). In her paper presented at the 1998 American Educational Research Association annual conference, Dr. Antonio Darder further described this armed love as "A love that could be lively, forceful, and inspiring, while at the same time, critical, challenging and insistent" (p. 497). Darder continues, "it is a love that I experienced as unconstricted, rooted in a committed willingness to struggle persistently with purpose in our life and to intimately connect that purpose with what he called our 'true vocation'—to be human" (p. 498).

As Freire speaks of the dangers of dehumanization, we think about the often unintentional structures of self-loathing that are present in our schools, in our books, and in the media. A pedagogy of revolutionary love must be motivated by a love of self. The books that we choose, the critical questions we ask of texts, the centering of our students as intellectuals, the centering of youth popular culture in our classrooms, the movement from curiosity to student-led projects, and the meaningful frameworks for family engagement all speak to a love of self. Only after we have promoted an awareness and a love of self can we turn our attention to the real joy of engaging and remaking this remarkable world we find ourselves in. The critical teaching of literature provides opportunities for the problem-posing and participatory work that allows our students to manifest their love for the world. In these moves, self-love and world-changing, we also hold up the power of literature and literacy for the agents of change we hope our children will become. These calls to self, community, and world are powerful motivators for the serious work we advocate in these chapters. Needless to say, we call for a re-languaging of the pedagogical act to include terms like joy, agency, responsiveness and love as we juxtapose them to children, to families, to literature, and to the classroom. We must renounce the language of risk, failure, and deficits as we contemplate the powerful and prominent role the teaching of literature can play in the fostering of the beloved literacy communities all classrooms should be.

REFERENCES

Children's and Young Adult Literature Referenced in the Book

Alexander, K. (2014). *The Crossover*. Boston: Houghton Mifflin Harcourt.

Alexander, K. (2019). *Undefeated*. New York: Houghton Mifflin Harcourt.

Anaya, R. (1972). *Bless Me, Ultima*. Berkeley, CA: TQS Publications.

Armento, B. (1999). *Oh, California*. (Level 4). Boston: Houghton Mifflin School.

Barnes, D. (2017). *Crown: An Ode to the Fresh Cut*. Evanston, IL: Denene Millner Books, Agate Publishing.

Behar, R. (2017). *Lucky Broken Girl*. New York: Nancy Paulson Books.

Bowie, C. W. (2002). *Busy Toes*. Watertown, MA: Charlesbridge Publishing.

Brown, M. (1947). *Goodnight Moon*. New York: Harper.

Bunting, E. (1999). *Smoky Night*. New York: Harcourt Brace & Co.

Bunting, E. (2006). *One green Apple*. New York: Clarion Books.

Chaucer, G. (1476). *Canterbury Tales*. England: William Caxton.

Choi, Y. (2003). *The Name Jar*. New York: Dell Dragonfly.

Cisneros, S. (1984). *The House on Mango Street*. New York: Vintage.

Coles, R. (1995). *The Story of Ruby Bridges*. New York: Scholastic Inc.

Creech, S. (1994). *Walk Two Moons*. New York: HarperCollins.

Curtis, C. P. (1995). *The Watsons Go to Birmingham—1963*. New York: Bantam Doubleday Dell Books for Young Readers.

Curtis, C. P. (1999). *Bud, Not Buddy*. New York: Delacorte Press.

Dahl, R. (1964). *Charlie and the Chocolate Factory*. New York: Alfred A. Knopf.

de la Peña, M. (2007). *Ball Don't Lie*. New York: Delacorte Press.

dePaola, T. (2004). *Adelita*. New York: Puffin Books.

Dickens, C. (1859). *Tale of Two Cities*. London: Chapman & Hall.

Dismondy, M. (2015). *Chocolate Milk, Por Favor*. Dearborn, MI: Making Spirits Bright; One Book at a Time.

Estes, E. (1944). *The Hundred Dresses*. New York: Harcourt, Brace.

Fitzgerald, F. S. (1925). *The Great Gatsby*. New York: Charles Scribner's Sons.

Flake, S. (2000). *The Skin I'm In*. New York: Jump at the Sun/ Hyperion Books for Children.

Fleischman, P. (1997). *Seedfolks*. New York: HarperCollins Publishers Inc.

Fleischman, S. (1986). *The Whipping Boy*. New York: Greenwillow Books.

Garza, C. L. (2000). *En Mi Familia*. San Francisco, CA: Children's Book Press.

Hawthorne, N. (1850). *The Scarlet Letter*. Boston: Ticknor, Reed & Fields.

Hesse, K. (2000). *Stowaway*. New York: Aladdin Paperback.

Hoana, B. (2019). *Navajo Code Talkers Top Secret Messengers of World War II*. Mankato, MN: Capstone Press.

Homer (1614). *The Odyssey*. George Chapman. [translation from eighth century BCE].

Kinney, J. (2007). *Diary of a Wimpy Kid*. New York: Amulet Books.

Lee, H. (1960). *To Kill a Mockingbird*. Philadelphia, PA: J. B. Lippincott & Co.

Lewis, C. S. (1950). *The Chronicles of Narnia*. New York: HarperCollins.

Lopez, D. (2018) *Lucky Luna*. New York: Scholastic.

Louie, A. (1982). *Yeh-Shen*. New York: Philomel Books.

Ludwig, T. (2004). *My Secret Bully*. Berkeley, CA: Tricycle Press.

Ludwig, T. (2006). *Sorry*. Berkeley, CA: Tricycle Press.

Martin, D. (1998). *The Rough Faced Girl*. New York: PaperStar Book.

McCain, B. (2001). *Nobody Knew What to Do: A Story about Bullying*. Park Ridge, IL: Albert Whitman & Company.

Miller, A. (1971). *The Crucible*. New York: Viking Press.

Morales, Y. (2018). *Dreamers*. New York: Neal Porter Books.

Myers, W. D. (1999). *Monster*. New York: HarperCollins Children's Books.

Munson, D. (2000). *Enemy Pie*. San Francisco, CA: Chronicle Books.

Numeroff, L. (1985). *If You Give a Mouse a Cookie*. New York: HarperCollins Publishers.

O'Brien, A. S. (2015). *I'm New Here*. Watertown, MA: Charlesbridge.

Oda, E. (2009). *One Piece: East Blue 1-2-3*. San Francisco, CA: VIZ Media LLC.

Rowling, J. K. (1997). *Harry Potter and the Philosopher's Stone*. New York: Scholastic Press.

Ryan, P. Munoz (2002). *Esperanza Rising*. New York: Scholastic.

Ryan, P. Munoz (2015). *Echo*. New York: Scholastic Books.

Saint-Exupery, A. (1943). *The Little Prince*. New York: Reynal & Hitchcock.

Saldaña, R. (2018). *The Curse of the Bully's Wrath/La maldición de la ira del abusón*. Houston, TX: Piñata Books.

Shakespeare, W. (1597). *Romeo and Juliet*. England: Cuthbert Burby.

Shakespeare, W. (1623). *MacBeth*. London: Edward Blount & William Jaggard.

Smith, S. (2018). *Who Were the Tuskegee Airmen?* New York: Penguin Workshop.

Steptoe, J. (1986). *Mufaro's Beautiful Daughters*. New York: HarperCollins Children's Books.

Takei, G. (2019). *They Called Us Enemy*. Marietta, GA: Top Shelf Productions.

Taylor, M. (1976). *Roll of Thunder, Hear My Cry*. New York: Dial Press.

Taylor, T. (1969). *The Cay*. New York: Avon.

Taylor, T. (1992). *The Cay*. Audiobook. Listening Library [Lavar Burton—reader].

Tolkien, J. R. R. (1968). *Lord of the Rings*. London: Allen & Unwin.

Twain, M. (1885). *The Adventures of Huckleberry Finn*. London: Chatto & Windus.

Walter, M. P. (1995). *Darkness*. New York: Simon and Schuster.

White, E. B. (1952). *Charlotte's Web*. New York: Harper and Brothers.

Whitman, A. (2001). *Nobody Knew What to Do: A Story about Bullying*. Park Ridge, IL: Albert Whitman & Company.

Wiesel, E. (1960). *Night*. New York: Hill & Wang [English translation].

Winter, J. (2009). *Nasreen's Secret School: A True Story from Afghanistan*. New York: Beach Lane Books.

Woods, C. (2014). *Tales from the Bully Box*. Springfield, NJ: Elephant's Bookshelf Press.

Woodson, J. (2014). *Brown Girl Dreaming*. New York: Penguin Group.

Woodson, J. (2018). *Harbor Me*. New York: Penguin Random House.

Yang, K. (2018). *Front Desk*. New York: Scholastic.

Zelver, P. (1996). *Wonderful Towers of Watts*. New York: Harper Trophy.

Adichi, C. N. (2009). *TEDTalks: The Dangers of a Single Story*. New York: Films Media Group.

Alim, S. (2006). *Roc the Mic Right: The Language of Hip Hop Culture*. New York: Routledge.

Allington, R. (2001). *What Really Matters for Struggling Readers: Designing Research-Based Programs*. New York: Addison Wesley Longman.

Allyn, P. & Morrell, E. (2016). *Every Child a Super Reader: Seven Strengths to Open a World of Possible*. New York: Scholastic.

Allyn, P. & Morrell, E. (2022). *Every Child a Super Reader: 7 Strengths for a Lifetime of Independence, Purpose and Joy* (2nd Ed.). New York: Scholastic.

Anderson, R., Hiebert, E., Scott, J. A. & Wilkinson, I. (1985). *Becoming a Nation of Readers: The Report of the Commission on Reading*. Washington, DC: National Academy of Education.

Anderson, R. C., Wilson, P. T. & Fielding, L. G. (1988). Growth in Reading and How Children Spend Their Time Outside of School. *Reading Research Quarterly, 23*, 285–303.

Anzaldua, G. (1987). *The Borderlands/La frontera: The New Mestiza*. San Francisco, CA: Aunt Lute Books.

Applebee, A. (1989). *A Study of Book-Length Works Taught in High School English Courses*. Albany, NY: Center for the Learning and Teaching of Literature.

Appleman, D. (2000). *Critical Encounters in High School English: Teaching Literary Theory to Adolescents (Language and Literacy Series)*. New York: Teachers College Press.

Appleman, D. (2015). *Critical Encounters in High School English: Teaching Literary Theory to Adolescents* (3rd Ed.). New York: Teachers College Press.

Armento, B. J., Nash, G. B., Salter, C. L. & Wixson, K. K. (1991). *Oh, California*. Boston: Houghton Mifflin.

Aronowitz, S. (2009). Foreword. In Sheila L. Macrine (Ed.) *Critical Pedagogy in Uncertain Times: Hope and Possibilities*. New York: Palgrave Macmillan.

Banks, J. A. (1978). Multiethnic education across cultures: United States, Mexico, Puerto Rico, France, and Great Britain. *Social Education, 42*, 177–85.

Banks, J. A. (Ed.) (1996). *Multicultural Education, Transformative Knowledge, and Action: Historical and Contemporary Perspectives*. New York: Teachers College Press.

Beers, K. & Probst, R. (2017). *Disrupting Thinking: Why How We Read Matters*. New York: Scholastic Inc.

Bishop, R. (1982). *Shadow and Substance: Afro-American Experience in Contemporary Children's Fiction*. Urbana, IL: National Council of Teachers of English.

Bishop, R. S. (1990). Mirrors, windows, and sliding glass doors. *Perspectives: Choosing and Using Books for the Classroom, 6*(3), ix–xi.

Boston Children's Hospital—Digital Wellness Lab (2022). What should I know about video games and kids? Retrieved from https://digitalwellnesslab.org/parents/video-games/

Botelho, M. J. & Rudman, M. K. (2009). *Critical Multicultural Analysis of Children's Literature*. New York: Routledge.

Bretherton, I. (1992). The origins of attachment theory: John Bowlby and Mary Ainsworth. *Developmental Psychology, 28*(5), 759–75.

Center for Disease Control and Prevention (2018). Screen time vs. lean time. Division of Nutrition, Physical Activity, and Obesity. Retrieved from https://www.cdc.gov/nccdphp/dnpao/multimedia/infographics/getmoving.html#:~:text=About%20Screen%20Time,watching%20a%20screen%20for%20fun

Chall, J. S., Jacobs, V. A. & Baldwin, L. E. (1990). *The Reading Crisis: Why Poor Children Fall Behind*. Cambridge, MA: Harvard University Press.

Chen, M. (2009). Seeking accurate cultural representation: Mahjong, World War II, and ethnic Chinese in multicultural youth literature. *Multicultural Education, 16*(3), 2–10.

Colabucci, L., Napoli, M., Ward, B. & Day, D. (2016). Children's book reviews: Putting the pleasure back into reading through read-alouds! *The Dragon Lode, 35*(1), 49–57.

Cooperative Children's Book Center (2022). Children's books by and/or about Black, Indigenous and People of Color received by the CCBC 2018. Retrieved from https://ccbc.education.wisc.edu/literature-resources/ccbc-diversity-statistics/

Copenhaver-Johnson, J. (2006). Talking to children about race: The importance of inviting difficult conversations. *Childhood Education, 83*(1), 12–22.

Csikszentmihalyi, M. (1990). *FLOW: The Psychology of Optimal Experience.* New York: Harper and Row.

Darder, A. (1998). *Teaching as an act of love: Reflections on Paulo Freire and his contributions to our lives and our work.* Paper presented at the annual meeting of the American Educational Research Association, San Diego, CA.

de los Ríos, C.V. (2019). "Los Músicos": Mexican corridos, the aural border, and the evocative musical renderings of transnational youth. *Harvard Educational Review, 89*(2), 177–200.

Dewey, J. (1899). *The School and Society.* Chicago, IL: The University of Chicago Press.

Dewey, J. (1901). *The Child and the Curriculum.* Chicago, IL: University of Chicago Press.

Dorn, L. & Soffos, C. (2005). *Teaching for Deep Comprehension: A Reading Workshop Approach.* Portsmouth, NH: Stenhouse Publishers.

Duke, N. (2010). Ask the expert. *Reading Teacher, 64*(3), 215.

Duke, N. & Bennett-Armistead, S. (2003). *Reading and Writing Informational Text in the Primary Grades.* New York: Scholastic.

Duncan-Andrade, J. & Morrell, E. (2008). *The Art of Critical Pedagogy: The Promise of Moving from Theory to Practice in Urban Schools.* New York: Peter Lang.

Emdin, C. (2016). *For White Folks Who Teach in the Hood … and the Rest of y'all too: Reality Pedagogy in Urban Education.* Boston: Beacon Press.

Fisher, M. (2007). *Writing in Rhythm: Spoken Word Poetry in Urban Classrooms.* New York: Teachers College Press.

Freire, P. (1970). *Pedagogy of the Oppressed.* New York: Bloomsbury Publishing.

Freire, P. (1997). *Teachers as Cultural Workers: Letters to Those Who Dare Teach.* New York: Routledge.

Freire, P. (1998). *The Paulo Freire Reader.* New York: Continuum.

Freire, P. & Macedo, D. (1987). *Literacy: Reading the Word and the World*. Westport, CT: Praeger.

Freire, P. & Macedo, D. (1995). A dialogue: Culture, language and race. *Harvard Educational Review*, 65(3), 377–402.

Gates, H. L. (1992). *Loose Canons: Notes on the Culture Wars*. Oxford: Oxford University Press.

Gates, H. L. (Ed.) (2002). *The Classic Slave Narratives*. New York: Signet Classics.

Gates, H. L. (Ed.) (2012). *The Slave Narratives*. New York: Signet Classics.

Gee, J. (2003). *What Video Games Have to Teach Us About Learning and Literacy*. New York: Palgrave-Macmillan.

Giroir, S., Grimaldo, L. Vaughn, S. & Roberst, G. (2015). Interactive read-alouds for English learners in the elementary grades. *The Reading Teachers*, 68(8), 639–48.

Giroux, H. A. (1990). Reading texts, literacy, and textual authority. *Journal of Education*, 172(1), 84–103.

Giroux, H. A. (2010). Rethinking education as the practice of freedom: Paulo Freire and the promise of critical pedagogy. *Policy Futures in Education*, 8(6), 715–21.

Giroux, H. A., and Pollock, G. (2010). *The Mouse That Roared: Disney and the End of Innocence*. Washington, DC: Rowman and Littlefield.

Graff, J. (2010). Countering narratives. *Teachers' Discourses about Immigrants and Their Experiences within the Realm of Children's and Young Adult Literature. English Teaching: Practice and Critique*, 91(3), 106–31.

Gutierrez, K. (2008). Developing a sociocritical literacy in the third space. *Reading Research Quarterly*, 43(2), 148–164.

Gutiérrez, K. D. & Rogoff, B. (2003). Cultural ways of learning: Individual traits or repertoires of practice. *Educational Researcher*, 32(5), 19–25.

Hamilton, V. (1989). Boston globe-horn book award. Acceptance Speech.

Harvey, S. (1998). *Nonfiction Matters*. Portland, ME: Stenhouse.

Heath, S. B. (1983). *Ways with Words: Language, Life and Work in Communities and Classrooms*. Cambridge, UK: Cambridge University Press.

International Literacy Association (2018). *The Power and Promise of Read-Alouds and Independent Reading* [Literacy leadership brief]. Newark, DE: Molly Ness.

Jensen, E., Jones, N., Rabe, M., Pratt, B., Medina, L., Orozco, K., Spell, L. (2021). *The Chance That Two People Chosen at Random Are of Different Race or Ethnicity Groups Has Increased since 2010*. Washington, DC: U.S. Census Bureau.

Kellner, D. (1995). *Cultural Studies, Identity and Politics: Between the Modern and the Postmodern*. New York: Routledge, 1–54.

Krashen, S. (2004). *The Power of Reading: Insights from the Research* (2nd Ed.). Portsmouth, NH: Heinemann.

Ladson-Billings, G. (1994). *The Dreamkeepers: Successful Teachers of African American Children*. Jossey-Bass: San Francisco.

Laminack, L. (2009). *Unwrapping the Read Aloud: Making Every Read Aloud Intentional and Instructional*. New York: Scholastic.

Laminack, L. & Wadsworth, R. (2012). *Bullying Hurts: Teaching Kindness through Read Alouds and Guided Conversations*. New York: Heinemann.

Landt, S. M. (2007). Weaving multicultural literature into middle school curricula. *Middle School Journal, 39*(2), 19–24.

Lankshear, C. & Knobel, M. (2003). *New Literacies: Changing Knowledge and Classroom Learning*. Philadelphia, PA: Open University Press.

Larrick, N. (1965). The All-White World of Children's Literature. *The Saturday Review, 48*, 63–65, 84–85.

Lee, C. D. (1993). *Signifying as a Scaffold for Literary Interpretation: The Pedagogical Implications of an African American Discourse Genre*. Urbana, IL: NCTE.

Loo, E. (2021). One Piece manga tops 490 million in circulation worldwide. Anime News Network.

Mapp, K. L. (2011). *Title I and parent involvement: Lessons from the past, recommendations for the future*. Conference paper prepared for the "Tightening Up Title I" symposium, Center for American Progress and the American Enterprise Institute. Washington D.C.

Mapp, K. L. & Kuttner, P. (2013). *Partners in Education: A Dual Capacity-Building Framework for Family–School Partnerships*. Washington, DC: US Department of Education.

Marcus, R. F. & Sanders-Reio, J. (2001). The influence of attachment on school completion. *School Psychology Quarterly, 16*(4), 427–44.

Martínez-Roldán, C. M. (2013). The representation of Latinos and the use of Spanish: A critical content analysis of Skippyjon Jones. *Journal of Children's Literature, 39*(1), 5–14.

Massaro, D. (2016). Two different communication genres and implications for vocabulary development and learning to read. *Journal of Literacy Research*, 47(4), 505–27.

Mirra, N., Garcia, A. & Morrell, E. (2016). *Doing Youth Participatory Action Research: Transforming Inquiry for Researchers, Educators, and Students*. New York: Routledge.

Mirra, N., Morrell, E. & Filipiak, D. (2018). From digital consumption to digital invention: Toward a critical theory and practice of multiliteracies. *Theory into Practice*, 57, 12–19.

Moll, L., Amanti, C., Neff, D. & Gonzalez, N. (1992). Funds of knowledge for teaching: Using a qualitative approach to connect homes and classrooms. *Theory into Practice, 31*(2), 132–41.

Morrell, E. (2003). English/Language arts curriculum revisited: Using court trials to teach writing in secondary english classrooms. *Florida English Journal, 39*(1), 20–2.

Morrell, E. (2008). Teaching became a revolution. In Sonia Nieto (Ed.) *Dear Paulo: Letters from Those Who Dare Teach* (pp. 102–103). Boulder, CO: Paradigm.

Morrell, E. & Morrell, J. (2012). Multicultural readings of multicultural literature and the promotion of social awareness in ELA classrooms. *New England Reading Association Journal*, 47(2), 10–16.

Morrell, E. & Morrell, J. (2021). Linking the word to the world: Connecting multicultural literature to the lives of 21st century youth. *Dragon Lode*.

Morrison, T. (1992). *Playing in the Dark: Whiteness and the Literary Imagination*. New York: Verso.

National Center for Education Statistics (2022). Fast facts: Back to school statistics. Retrieved February 8, 2023, from https://nces.ed.gov/fastfacts/display.asp?id=372

National Center for Education Statistics (2022). Concentration of public school students eligible for free or reduced-price lunch. Retrieved February 8, 2023, from https://nces.ed.gov/programs/coe/indicator/clb/free-or-reduced-price-lunch#:~:text=In%20fall%202019%2C%20about%2012.3,students%20attended%20high%2Dpoverty%20schools

National Center for Education Statistics (2022). Racial/Ethnic enrollment in public schools. Retrieved February 8, 2023, from https://nces.ed.gov/programs/coe/indicator/cge/racial-ethnic-enrollment

National School Climate Center, Center for Social and
Emotional Education, and National Center for Learning
and Citizenship at the Education Commission of the States
(2008). *The School Climate Challenge: Narrowing the
Gap between School Climate Research and School Climate
Policy, Practice Guidelines and Teacher Education Policy.*
Retrieved February 8, 2023, from http://www.ecs.org/html/
projectsPartners/nclc/docs/schoo-climate-challenge-web.pdf

New American Economy (2021). Combatting the AAPI perpetual
foreigner stereotype. Retrieved from https://research.
newamericaneconomy.org/report/aapi-perpetual-foreigner-
stereotype/

New London Group (1996). A pedagogy of multiliteracies: Designing
social futures. *Harvard Educational Review*, 66(1), 60–92.

Pagan, A. (2018). *A Beginner's Guide to Manga.* UK: New
York Public Library. Retrieved from https://www.nypl.org/
blog/2018/12/27/beginners-guide-manga

Paley, V. (2000). *White Teacher.* Cambridge, MA: Harvard
University Press.

Paulson, E. J. & Armstrong, S. L. (2010). Situating reader stance
within and beyond the efferent-aesthetic continuum. *Literacy
Research and Instruction*, 49, 86–97.

Reading Rockets (2015). *Mirrors, Windows and Sliding Glass
Doors* [Video]. https://www.youtube.com/watch?v=_
AAu58SNSyc&t=12s

Reynolds, K. (2011). *Children's Literature: A Very Short
Introduction.* Oxford: Oxford University Press.

Rivero, E. & Gutiérrez, K. D. (2022). Children Learning by Observing
and Pitching in to community endeavors in online gaming
communities (Los niños Aprenden por medio de Observary
Acomedirse a las actividades de la comunidad en los juegos en
línea). *Journal for the Study of Education and Development*,
45(3), 701–10. DOI: 10.1080/02103702.2022.2062902

Rosenblatt, L. (1938). *Literature as Exploration.* New York:
D. Appleton Company.

Rosenblatt, L. (1978). *The Reader, the Text, and the Poem: The
Transactional Theory of the Literary Work.* Carbondale, IL:
Southern Illinois University Press.

Routman, R. (2003). *Reading Essentials: The Specifics You Need to
Teach Reading Well.* Portsmouth, NH: Heinemann.

Salas, R., Lucido, F. & Canales, J. (2002). *Multicultural Literature: Broadening Young Children's Experiences.* (Report No. ED-468 866) Texas A&M Early Childhood Development Center. Retrieved from ERIC Database.

Schaeffer, K. (2021). *Among Many U.S. Children, Reading for Fun has Become Less Common, Federal Data Shows.* Washington, DC: Pew Research Center.

Scholastic (2019). *Kids and Family Reading Report: Finding Their Story* (7th Ed.). New York: Scholastic.

Scribner, S. & Cole, M. (1981). *The Psychology of Literacy.* Cambridge, MA: Harvard University Press.

Selman, R. (2003). *The Promotion of Social Awareness: Powerful Lessons from the Partnership of Developmental Theory and Classroom Practice.* New York: Russell Sage.

Shannon, P. (2016). The struggle for pleasure in reading at school. *The Dragon Lode, 31*(1), 36–39.

Snow, C., Burns, M.S. & Griffin, P. (Eds.) (1998). *Preventing Reading Difficulties in Young Children.* Washington, DC: National Academy Press.

Snow, C., Griffin, P. & Burns, S. (Eds.) (2005). *Knowledge to Support the Teaching of Reading: Preparing Teachers for a Changing World.* New York: Jossey-Bass.

Solórzano, D. & Yosso, T. (2002). A critical race counterstory of race, racism, and affirmative action. *Equity and Excellence in Education, 35*(2), 155–68.

Souto Manning, M. (2004). Circles of culture: Literacy as a process for social inclusion. *Colombian Applied Linguistics Journal,* (6), 23–41. Retrieved July 24, 2022, from http://www.scielo.org.co/scielo.php?script=sci_arttext&pid=S0123-46412004000100002&lng=en&tlng=en

Souto-Manning, M. (2010). *Freire, Teaching, and Learning: Culture Circles across Contexts.* New York: Peter Lang.

Stallworth, J. (2012). What's on the list … now? A survey of book-length works taught in secondary schools. *English Leadership Quarterly, 34*(3), 2–3.

Statistics & Data (2022). Most popular manga of all time. Retrieved February 8, 2023, from https://statisticsanddata.org/data/most-popular-manga-of-all-time/

Steinberg, S. (Ed.) (2011). *Kinderculture: The Corporate Construction of Childhood.* New York: Routledge.

Street, B. (1984). *Literacy in Theory and Practice*. Cambridge: Cambridge University Press.

Sutherland, R. (1985). Hidden persuaders: Political ideologies in literature for children. *Children's Literature in Education, 16*(3), 143–57.

Thomas, E. E. (2016). Stories *still* matter: Rethinking the role of diverse children's literature today. *Language Arts, 94*(2), 112–19.

Tompkins, G. (2006). *Literacy for the 21st Century: A Balanced Approach* (5th Ed.). New Jersey: Merrill Prentice Hall.

Torres, C. A. (2014). *First Freire: Early Writings in Social Justice Education*. New York: Teachers College Press.

U.S. Department of Education, National Center for Education Statistics (2010). Common Core of Data (CCD), "State nonfiscal survey of public elementary/secondary education," 1994–95 through 2007–08; and National Public Elementary and Secondary Enrollment by Race/Ethnicity Model, 1994–2007. (This table was prepared January 2010.)

Vygotsky, L. (1978). *Mind in Society: The Development of Higher Psychological Processes*. Cambridge, MA: Harvard University Press.

Wanless, S. & Crawford, P. (2016). Reading your way to a culturally responsive classroom. *Young Children, 71*(2), 8–15.

Wilhelm, J. (1997). *You Gotta Be the Book: Teaching Engaged and Reflective Reading with Adolescents*. New York: Teachers College Press.

Wilhelm, J. (2016). *You Gotta Be the Book: Teaching Engaged and Reflective Reading with Adolescents*. New York: Teachers College Press.

Wilhelm, J. & Wilhelm, P. (2010). Inquiring minds learn to read, write, and think: Reaching all learners through inquiry. *Middle School Journal, 41*(5), 39–46.

Yokota, J. (2001). *Kaleidoscope: A Multicultural Booklist for Grades K-8* (3rd Ed.). Urbana, IL: National Council of Teachers of English.

Yoon, B. Simpson, A. & Haag, C. (2010). Assimilation ideology: Critically examining underlying messages in multicultural literature. *Journal of Adolescent & Adult Literacy, 54*(2), 109–18.

Zinn, H. (1995). *A People's History of the United States: 1492–Present*. New York: HarperCollins Publishers, Inc.

INDEX